Search and Rescue

Canine

Training Log and Journal

- **Search and Rescue Canine Training Log and Journal**

By J. C. Judah

Second Edition. 8 X 10 in. Size.

C. 2009 by J. C. Judah. All rights reserved. No copy of any contents may be reproduced without the express written permission of the author.

Published by Coastal Books.

Contact: 2690 Ocean Station SW, Supply, NC 28462. (910) 842-7942.

EAN-13　　978-1-4421-3245-0
ISBN　　　1442132450

Books by this Author:

Search and Rescue Training Log and Journal (for Non-dog handlers)
Building a Basic Foundation for Search and Rescue Dog Training
An Ancient History of Dogs: Spaniels through the Ages

The Faircloth Family Genealogy Resource Guide
Faircloth Family Genealogy: William Faircloth I Lineage
Faircloth Family Genealogy: Edward Farecloth Lineage

Buzzards and Butterflies: Human Remains Detection Dogs
The Legends of Brunswick County: Ghosts, Pirates, Indians and Colonial North Carolina

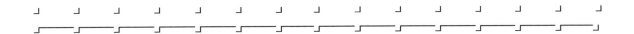

Search and Rescue Canine Training Log and Journal

J. C. Judah

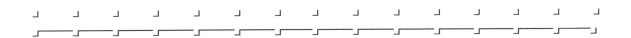

Preface

All handlers are expected and encouraged to maintain accurate training records for use in evaluating their current training status and formulating future training plans. This manual has been formulated to assist the handler in the documentation of training and mission experiences. The journal is presented in multiple sections to facilitate the documentation of canine and handler information and provide a process for routine documentation.

Table of Contents

Section One – Handler Documentation 1

    I. Demographics 1

    II. Certifications 2

        A. SAR Certifications 2

        B. Handler Specialties/Certifications 3

        C. Seminars/Workshops/Conferences/Specialty Training 4

Section Two – Canine Documentation 5

    I. Demographics 5

    II. Canine Health Information 6

        A. Heartworm Prevention 6

        B. Flea/Tick Treatment Prevention 6

        C. Immunization Records 6

        D. Health Information – Injury or Illness, Surgeries, etc. 7

    III. Canine Certifications/Seminars/Workshops Attended 8

        A. Certifications/Credentials 8

        B. Seminars/Workshops/ Specialty Training 9

Section Three – Objectives and Goals 11

    I. Objectives/Goals: 11

    II. Environmental Scenarios 16

        A. Live / Air Scent 16

        B. Human Remains Detection 17

        C. Water Recovery 18

        D. Trailing 19

        E. Obedience / Agility 20

Section Four – Training Logs 21

    I. Training Summary Log 21

    II. SAR Canine Training Log / Journal 26

Section Five - SAR Mission Logs 131

        A. Log Summary 131

        B. Mission Summaries 133

Section Six - Memories 147

Section One
Handler Documentation

Name of Handler: _____
                          First   Middle   Last

(Insert Photograph)

I. Demographics

DOB:_____ Home Phone:_____

Emergency Notification:

*Name:_____

Address:_____
_____

Home Phone:_____ Cell Phone:_____
Pager:_____ Work Phone:_____

*Name:_____

Address:_____
_____

Home Phone:_____ Cell Phone:_____
Pager:_____ Work Phone:_____

II. Certifications

A. SAR Certifications

Date   **Certification**

B. Handler Specialties/Certifications: (Medical, CPR, EMT, Amateur Radio License, fire, Water Rescue, etc.)

Date　　　　　　　　　　**Certification**

C. Seminars/workshops/Conferences/Specialty Training:

Date   **Name/Location**

Section Two

Canine Documentation

Name of Canine:_____

(Insert Photograph)

I. Demographics

    A. Date of Birth:_____   **B. Sex:** male   female

    B. Canine Registry #: (AKC, UKC, CKC, etc.)_____

    C. Tatoo: _____

    D. Microchip ID: Company:_____ #:_____

    E. Description:
Breed:_____
Color:_____
Markings:_____
Scars:_____

Weight: _____ (Date:_____)
Weight: _____ (Date:_____)
Weight: _____ (Date:_____)
Weight: _____ (Date:_____)
Weight: _____ (Date:_____)
Weight: _____ (Date:_____)

II. Canine Health Information

A. Heartworm Prevention:

B. Flea/Tick Treatment Prevention:

C. Immunization Records:
(Rabies, Distemper, Hepatitis, Leptospirosis, Parvovirus, Parainfluenza, Coronovirus, Bordetella, etc.

Date	Age	Immunization	Administered By

D. Health Information – Injury or Illness, Surgeries, etc.

Date	Event	Medications

III. Canine Certifications/Seminars/Workshops Attended

A. Certifications/Credentials

1. Date:_____   Name of Dog:_____   Handler:_____

Name of Certifying Agency:_____
Name of Individual Certifying K9:_____
Type of
Certification:_____
Renewal date:_____

2. Date:_____   Name of Dog:_____   Handler:_____

Name of Certifying Agency:_____
Name of Individual Certifying K9:_____
Type of
Certification:_____
Renewal date:_____

3. Date:_____   Name of Dog:_____   Handler:_____

Name of Certifying Agency:_____
Name of Individual Certifying K9:_____
Type of
Certification:_____
Renewal date:_____

4. Date:_____   Name of Dog:_____   Handler:_____

Name of Certifying Agency:_____
Name of Individual Certifying K9:_____
Type of
Certification:_____
Renewal date:_____

5. Date:_____   Name of Dog:_____   Handler:_____

Name of Certifying Agency:_____
Name of Individual Certifying K9:_____
Type of
Certification:_____
Renewal date:_____

B. Seminars/Workshops/ Specialty Training

Date   **Name / Location / Instructor (s) / Hosting Agency**

Section Three

Training Objectives/Goals

I. Objectives/Goals:
All goals should be SMART: Specific, Measurable, Action Oriented, Realistic, & Time Sensitive.

Goal:_____
_____
_____
_____
_____
_____
_____

Date Set:_____ Target Date:_____ Date Achieved:_____

Goal:_____
_____
_____
_____
_____
_____

Date Set:_____ Target Date:_____ Date Achieved:_____

Goal:_____
_____
_____
_____
_____
_____
_____

Date Set:_____ Target Date:_____ Date Achieved:_____

Goal:_____
_____
_____
_____
_____
_____

Date Set:_____ Target Date:_____ Date Achieved:_____

Goal:_____
_____
_____
_____
_____

Date Set:_____ Target Date:_____ Date Achieved:_____

Goal:_____
_____
_____
_____
_____
_____

Date Set:_____ Target Date:_____ Date Achieved:_____

Goal:_____
_____
_____
_____
_____

Date Set:_____ Target Date:_____ Date Achieved:_____

Goal:_____
_____
_____
_____
_____
_____
_____

Date Set:_____ Target Date:_____ Date Achieved:_____

Goal:_____
_____
_____
_____
_____
_____
_____

Date Set:_____ Target Date:_____ Date Achieved:_____

Goal:_____
_____
_____
_____
_____
_____
_____

Date Set:_____ Target Date:_____ Date Achieved:_____

Goal:_____
_____
_____
_____
_____
_____
_____

Date Set:_____ Target Date:_____ Date Achieved:_____

Goal:_____
_____
_____
_____
_____

Date Set:_____ Target Date:_____ Date Achieved:_____

Goal:_____
_____
_____
_____
_____
_____
_____

Date Set:_____ Target Date:_____ Date Achieved:_____

Goal:_____
_____
_____
_____
_____
_____
_____

Date Set:_____ Target Date:_____ Date Achieved:_____

Goal:_____
_____
_____
_____
_____
_____
_____

Date Set:_____ Target Date:_____ Date Achieved:_____

Goal:_____
_____
_____
_____
_____

Date Set:_____ Target Date:_____ Date Achieved:_____

Goal:_____
_____
_____
_____
_____
_____
_____

Date Set:_____ Target Date:_____ Date Achieved:_____

Goal:_____
_____
_____
_____
_____
_____
_____

Date Set:_____ Target Date:_____ Date Achieved:_____

Goal:_____
_____
_____
_____
_____
_____
_____

Date Set:_____ Target Date:_____ Date Achieved:_____

II. Environmental Scenarios

A. Live / Air Scent

Scenario_____**Date(s)**_____

Single victim _____
Multiple victims_____
Stationary victim (s)_____
Moving victim (s)_____
Concealed victim_____
Sitting victim _____
Prone victim _____
Evading victim_____
Deceased victim_____
Urban setting _____
Rural setting _____
Wilderness setting_____
Shopping Ctr/Mall_____
Overhead victim_____
Unconscious victim_____
Injured victim _____
Inside Building_____
Minor Rubble _____
Major Rubble _____
In Water/River/Pond_____
Hills/Mountains_____
Sand/Desert _____
Park _____
Negative Area _____
Age:_____
Race:_____
_____
_____
_____
_____
_____
_____
_____
_____
_____
_____
_____

B. Human Remains Detection

Scenario _____ **Date(s)** _____

Open view _____
Lightly covered w/leaves _____
Covered with other object _____
Buried 2 inches _____
Buried 4 inches _____
Buried 6 inches _____
Buried 12 inches _____
Buried 18 inches _____
Hanging, 5 feet _____
Hanging, 10 feet _____
Negative area _____
Gravesite date:
    Age:_____ _____
    Age:_____ _____
    Age:_____ _____
    Age:_____ _____
    Age:_____ _____
    Age:_____ _____
    Age:_____ _____
    Age:_____ _____
    Age:_____ _____
    Age:_____ _____
    Age:_____ _____
    Age:_____ _____
    Age:_____ _____
    Age:_____ _____
    Age:_____ _____

Sample Type:
    Age: _____ Type:_____ Date (s):_____
    Age: _____ Type:_____ Date (s):_____
    Age: _____ Type:_____ Date (s):_____
    Age: _____ Type:_____ Date (s):_____
    Age: _____ Type:_____ Date (s):_____
    Age: _____ Type:_____ Date (s):_____
    Age: _____ Type:_____ Date (s):_____
    Age: _____ Type:_____ Date (s):_____
    Age: _____ Type:_____ Date (s):_____
    Age: _____ Type:_____ Date (s):_____

Other:_____

C. Water Recovery

Scenario **Date (s)** _____

Fresh Water _____
Salt Water _____
Swift Water _____
Pond _____
River _____
Lake _____
Ocean _____
Inland Waterway _____
Bay _____
Still Water _____
Marsh Land _____
Creek _____
_____ _____

Dock _____
Pier _____
Shoreline _____

Water Depth   **Temperatures**   **Depth of Source**

_____   _____   _____
_____   _____   _____
_____   _____   _____
_____   _____   _____
_____   _____   _____
_____   _____   _____

Sample Used:

_____   _____
_____   _____
_____   _____
_____   _____
_____   _____

Other:

_____
_____
_____
_____

D. Trailing

Scenario	Date (s)
Daylight	
Night	
AM	
PM	
Residential	
Urban	
Apt Complex	
Building	
Business	
Shopping/Mall	
School	
Park	
Blocked Entry	
Street	
Highway	
Alleyway	
Dirt Road	
Gravel Road	
Concrete	
Asphalt	
Sand	
Clay	
Dirt	
Rocky	
Grass	
Brush	
Woods	
Thick/Heavy	
Thin/Light	
Flat	
Hilly	
Cross Creek	
Cross River	
Marsh	
Vehicle Trail	
4/wheeler trail	
Fresh: 1-4 hrs	
Aged 4 hrs	
Aged 8 hrs	
Aged 12 hrs	
Aged 18 hrs	
Aged 24 hrs	
Aged 48 hrs	

Aged 72 hrs _____
Aged ___ hrs _____
Aged ___ hrs _____

E. Obedience / Agility

Sit _____
Sit/Stay _____
Down _____
Down / Stay _____
Loose Heel _____
Come _____
Check It _____
Leave It _____
Loose _____
Wait _____
Load _____
Stand for Exam _____

Over _____
Under _____
Through/Tunnel _____
Ladder _____
Wobbly Surface _____
Raised Surface _____
Low Planks _____
Cat Walk _____
Pause Boxes _____
Directionals _____
Rubble Work _____
Disaster House _____
Stairs _____
Slippery Surfaces _____
Weave Poles/Tight Work _____

_____
_____
_____
_____
_____
_____
_____
_____
_____
_____
_____

Section Four

Training Logs

I. Training Summary Log

Date	Location	Focus of Training

Date	Location	Focus of Training

Date	Location	Focus of Training

Date **Location** **Focus of Training**

Date	Location	Focus of Training

II. SAR Canine Training Log / Journal

K9:_____ Handler:_____
Date:_____
Location:_____
Mileage: Beginning:_____ Ending:_____ Total:_____
Beginning Time: _____ Ending Time:_____ Total:_____

Conditions:
Wind Speed:_____ Wind Direction:_____ Humidity:_____ Temperature:_____
Cloud Cover:_____ Shadow (ft): _____ Other:_____
Rain:__ Hail:__ Snow:__ Sleet: __ Other:_____

Environment:
___Grass ___Brush ___Timber ___Level
___Rolling ___Steep ___Thick ___Thin
___Moderate ___Rubble ___Ext. Building ___Residential
___Clpsed Structure ___Inter. Bld. ___Commercial ___Industrial
___Lake ___Pond ___River ___Creek
___From boat ___From Shore

___ _____
___ _____
___ _____

Size of Search Area/Length of Trail:_____

Age of Exercise (i.e. hrs, days, etc):_____
Scent Article Used:_____ **Age of Scent Article**:_____

Type of Exercise/Training:
___Agility ___Directional ___Obedience
___Socialization ___Area Search ___Area Search w/ Pop-Up
___Runaway reps ___Trail ___Area Search w/ Callout
___HRD ___Water Recovery ___Disaster ___ Indication/Alert

Training Subjects:
___Location Known to handler ___ Location Unknown to Handler
___Live/Mobile ___Live/Immobile ___Live/Concealed ___Live/Bizarre

Behavior _____

Victim Description: ___Age ___Race ___Weight
___Gender ___Height ___Other

HRD:
___HRD / Visible ___HRD / Concealed ___HRD / Overhead ___HRD / Buried

HRD Sample Type/Age:
_____
_____

Sketch of Search Area and Exercise:

Comments: (Include evaluation of performance, plans for next training session, weaknesses, strengths.)

K9:_____ Handler:_____
Date:_____ _____
Location:_____
Mileage: Beginning:_____ Ending:_____ Total:_____
Beginning Time: _____ Ending Time:_____ Total:_____

Conditions:
Wind Speed:_____ Wind Direction:_____ Humidity:_____ Temperature:_____
Cloud Cover:_____ Shadow (ft): _____ Other:_____
Rain:__ Hail:__ Snow:__ Sleet: __ Other:_____

Environment:
___Grass ___Brush ___Timber ___Level
___Rolling ___Steep ___Thick ___Thin
___Moderate ___Rubble ___Ext. Building ___Residential
___Clpsed Structure ___Inter. Bld. ___Commercial ___Industrial
___Lake ___Pond ___River ___Creek
___From boat ___From Shore

___ _____
___ _____
___ _____

Size of Search Area/Length of Trail:_____

Age of Exercise (i.e. hrs, days, etc):_____
Scent Article Used:_____ **Age of Scent Article**:_____

Type of Exercise/Training:
___Agility ___Directional ___Obedience
___Socialization ___Area Search ___Area Search w/ Pop-Up
___Runaway reps ___Trail ___Area Search w/ Callout
___HRD ___Water Recovery ___Disaster ___ Indication/Alert

Training Subjects:
___Location Known to handler ___ Location Unknown to Handler
___Live/Mobile ___Live/Immobile ___Live/Concealed ___Live/Bizarre

Behavior _____

Victim Description: ____Age _____Race _____Weight
____Gender ____Height _____Other

HRD:
___HRD / Visible ___HRD / Concealed ___HRD / Overhead ___HRD / Buried
HRD Sample Type/Age:

_____
_____

Sketch of Search Area and Exercise:

Comments: (Include evaluation of performance, plans for next training session, weaknesses, strengths.)

K9:_____   Handler:_____
Date:_____
Location:_____
Mileage: Beginning:_____Ending:_____Total:_____
Beginning Time: _____Ending Time:_____ Total:_____

Conditions:
Wind Speed:_____ Wind Direction:_____ Humidity:_____ Temperature:_____
Cloud Cover:_____ Shadow (ft): _____ Other:_____
Rain:__ Hail:__ Snow:__ Sleet: __ Other:_____

Environment:
___Grass   ___Brush   ___Timber   ___Level
___Rolling   ___Steep   ___Thick   ___Thin
___Moderate   ___Rubble   ___Ext. Building ___Residential
___Clpsed Structure ___Inter. Bld. ___Commercial   ___Industrial
___Lake   ___Pond   ___River   ___Creek
___From boat   ___From Shore
___ _____
___ _____
___ _____

Size of Search Area/Length of Trail:_____

Age of Exercise (i.e. hrs, days, etc):_____
Scent Article Used:_____**Age of Scent Article**:_____

Type of Exercise/Training:
___Agility   ___Directional   ___Obedience
___Socialization ___Area Search   ___Area Search w/ Pop-Up
___Runaway reps ___Trail   ___Area Search w/ Callout
___HRD   ___Water Recovery ___Disaster   ___ Indication/Alert

Training Subjects:
___Location Known to handler   ___ Location Unknown to Handler
___Live/Mobile   ___Live/Immobile   ___Live/Concealed   ___Live/Bizarre

Behavior _____

Victim Description: ___Age   ___Race   ___Weight
                      ___Gender   ___Height   ___Other
HRD:
___HRD / Visible   ___HRD / Concealed___HRD / Overhead___HRD / Buried
HRD Sample Type/Age:
_____
_____

Sketch of Search Area and Exercise:

Comments: (Include evaluation of performance, plans for next training session, weaknesses, strengths.)

K9:_____   Handler:_____
Date:_____
Location:_____
Mileage: Beginning:_____ Ending:_____ Total:_____
Beginning Time: _____ Ending Time:_____ Total:_____

Conditions:
Wind Speed:_____ Wind Direction:_____ Humidity:_____ Temperature:_____
Cloud Cover:_____ Shadow (ft): _____ Other:_____
Rain:__ Hail:__ Snow:__ Sleet: __ Other:_____

Environment:
___Grass   ___Brush   ___Timber   ___Level
___Rolling   ___Steep   ___Thick   ___Thin
___Moderate   ___Rubble   ___Ext. Building   ___Residential
___Clpsed Structure ___Inter. Bld. ___Commercial   ___Industrial
___Lake   ___Pond   ___River   ___Creek
___From boat   ___From Shore

___ _____
___ _____
___ _____

Size of Search Area/Length of Trail:_____

Age of Exercise (i.e. hrs, days, etc):_____
Scent Article Used:_____ **Age of Scent Article**:_____

Type of Exercise/Training:
___Agility   ___Directional   ___Obedience
___Socialization   ___Area Search   ___Area Search w/ Pop-Up
___Runaway reps   ___Trail   ___Area Search w/ Callout
___HRD   ___Water Recovery   ___Disaster   ___ Indication/Alert

Training Subjects:
___Location Known to handler   ___ Location Unknown to Handler
___Live/Mobile   ___Live/Immobile   ___Live/Concealed   ___Live/Bizarre

Behavior _____

Victim Description: ___Age   ___Race   ___Weight
                     ___Gender   ___Height   ___Other

HRD:
___HRD / Visible   ___HRD / Concealed   ___HRD / Overhead   ___HRD / Buried
HRD Sample Type/Age:
_____
_____

Sketch of Search Area and Exercise:

Comments: (Include evaluation of performance, plans for next training session, weaknesses, strengths.)

K9:_____ Handler:_____
Date:_____
Location:_____
Mileage: Beginning:_____Ending:_____Total:_____
Beginning Time: _____Ending Time:_____ Total:_____

Conditions:
Wind Speed:_____ Wind Direction:_____ Humidity:_____ Temperature:_____
Cloud Cover:_____ Shadow (ft): _____ Other:_____
Rain:__ Hail:__ Snow:__ Sleet: __ Other:_____

Environment:
___Grass ___Brush ___Timber ___Level
___Rolling ___Steep ___Thick ___Thin
___Moderate ___Rubble ___Ext. Building ___Residential
___Clpsed Structure ___Inter. Bld. ___Commercial ___Industrial
___Lake ___Pond ___River ___Creek
___From boat ___From Shore

___ _____
___ _____
___ _____

Size of Search Area/Length of Trail:_____

Age of Exercise (i.e. hrs, days, etc):_____
Scent Article Used:_____**Age of Scent Article**:_____

Type of Exercise/Training:
___Agility ___Directional ___Obedience
___Socialization ___Area Search ___Area Search w/ Pop-Up
___Runaway reps ___Trail ___Area Search w/ Callout
___HRD ___Water Recovery ___Disaster ___ Indication/Alert

Training Subjects:
___Location Known to handler ___ Location Unknown to Handler
___Live/Mobile ___Live/Immobile ___Live/Concealed ___Live/Bizarre

Behavior _____

Victim Description: ___Age ___Race ___Weight
___Gender ___Height ___Other
HRD:
___HRD / Visible ___HRD / Concealed ___HRD / Overhead ___HRD / Buried
HRD Sample Type/Age:
_____
_____

Sketch of Search Area and Exercise:

Comments: (Include evaluation of performance, plans for next training session, weaknesses, strengths.)

K9:_____ Handler:_____
Date:_____ _____
Location:_____
Mileage: Beginning:_____ Ending:_____ Total:_____
Beginning Time: _____ Ending Time:_____ Total:_____

Conditions:
Wind Speed:_____ Wind Direction:_____ Humidity:_____ Temperature:_____
Cloud Cover:_____ Shadow (ft): _____ Other:_____
Rain:__ Hail:__ Snow:__ Sleet:__ Other:_____

Environment:
___Grass   ___Brush   ___Timber   ___Level
___Rolling   ___Steep   ___Thick   ___Thin
___Moderate   ___Rubble   ___Ext. Building ___Residential
___Clpsed Structure ___Inter. Bld. ___Commercial   ___Industrial
___Lake   ___Pond   ___River   ___Creek
___From boat   ___From Shore
___ _____
___ _____
___ _____

Size of Search Area/Length of Trail:_____

Age of Exercise (i.e. hrs, days, etc):_____
Scent Article Used:_____ **Age of Scent Article**:_____

Type of Exercise/Training:
___Agility   ___Directional   ___Obedience
___Socialization ___Area Search   ___Area Search w/ Pop-Up
___Runaway reps ___Trail   ___Area Search w/ Callout
___HRD   ___Water Recovery   ___Disaster   ___Indication/Alert

Training Subjects:
___Location Known to handler   ___Location Unknown to Handler
___Live/Mobile   ___Live/Immobile   ___Live/Concealed   ___Live/Bizarre

Behavior _____

Victim Description: ___Age   ___Race   ___Weight
                     ___Gender   ___Height   ___Other
HRD:
___HRD / Visible   ___HRD / Concealed   ___HRD / Overhead   ___HRD / Buried
HRD Sample Type/Age:
_____
_____

Sketch of Search Area and Exercise:

Comments: (Include evaluation of performance, plans for next training session, weaknesses, strengths.)

K9:_____ Handler:_____
Date:_____
Location:_____
Mileage: Beginning:_____Ending:_____Total:_____
Beginning Time: _____Ending Time:_____ Total:_____

Conditions:
Wind Speed:_____ Wind Direction:_____ Humidity:_____ Temperature:_____
Cloud Cover:_____ Shadow (ft): _____ Other:_____
Rain:__ Hail:__ Snow:__ Sleet: __ Other:_____

Environment:
___Grass   ___Brush   ___Timber   ___Level
___Rolling   ___Steep   ___Thick   ___Thin
___Moderate   ___Rubble   ___Ext. Building ___Residential
___Clpsed Structure ___Inter. Bld. ___Commercial   ___Industrial
___Lake   ___Pond   ___River   ___Creek
___From boat   ___From Shore

___ _____
___ _____
___ _____

Size of Search Area/Length of Trail:_____

Age of Exercise (i.e. hrs, days, etc):_____
Scent Article Used:_____**Age of Scent Article**:_____

Type of Exercise/Training:
___Agility   ___Directional   ___Obedience
___Socialization   ___Area Search   ___Area Search w/ Pop-Up
___Runaway reps   ___Trail   ___Area Search w/ Callout
___HRD   ___Water Recovery   ___Disaster   ___ Indication/Alert

Training Subjects:
___Location Known to handler   ___ Location Unknown to Handler
___Live/Mobile   ___Live/Immobile   ___Live/Concealed   ___Live/Bizarre

Behavior _____

Victim Description: ____Age   ____Race   ____Weight
                     ____Gender   ____ Height   ____Other
HRD:
___HRD / Visible   ___HRD / Concealed ___HRD / Overhead ___HRD / Buried
HRD Sample Type/Age:
_____
_____

Sketch of Search Area and Exercise:

Comments: (Include evaluation of performance, plans for next training session, weaknesses, strengths.)

K9:_____ Handler:_____
Date:_____
Location:_____
Mileage: Beginning:_____Ending:_____Total:_____
Beginning Time: _____Ending Time:_____ Total:_____

Conditions:
Wind Speed:_____ Wind Direction:_____ Humidity:_____ Temperature:_____
Cloud Cover:_____ Shadow (ft): _____ Other:_____
Rain:__ Hail:__ Snow:__ Sleet: __ Other:_____

Environment:
___Grass ___Brush ___Timber ___Level
___Rolling ___Steep ___Thick ___Thin
___Moderate ___Rubble ___Ext. Building ___Residential
___Clpsed Structure ___Inter. Bld. ___Commercial ___Industrial
___Lake ___Pond ___River ___Creek
___From boat ___From Shore

___ _____
___ _____
___ _____

Size of Search Area/Length of Trail:_____

Age of Exercise (i.e. hrs, days, etc):_____
Scent Article Used:_____**Age of Scent Article**:_____

Type of Exercise/Training:
___Agility ___Directional ___Obedience
___Socialization ___Area Search ___Area Search w/ Pop-Up
___Runaway reps ___Trail ___Area Search w/ Callout
___HRD ___Water Recovery ___Disaster ___ Indication/Alert

Training Subjects:
___Location Known to handler ___ Location Unknown to Handler
___Live/Mobile ___Live/Immobile ___Live/Concealed ___Live/Bizarre

Behavior _____

Victim Description: ___Age ___Race ___Weight
 ___Gender ___Height ___Other
HRD:
___HRD / Visible ___HRD / Concealed ___HRD / Overhead ___HRD / Buried
HRD Sample Type/Age:
_____
_____

Sketch of Search Area and Exercise:

Comments: (Include evaluation of performance, plans for next training session, weaknesses, strengths.)

K9:_____ Handler:_____
Date:_____
Location:_____
Mileage: Beginning:_____ Ending:_____ Total:_____
Beginning Time: _____ Ending Time:_____ Total:_____

Conditions:
Wind Speed:_____ Wind Direction:_____ Humidity:_____ Temperature:_____
Cloud Cover:_____ Shadow (ft): _____ Other:_____
Rain:__ Hail:__ Snow:__ Sleet: __ Other:_____

Environment:
___Grass   ___Brush   ___Timber   ___Level
___Rolling   ___Steep   ___Thick   ___Thin
___Moderate   ___Rubble   ___Ext. Building ___Residential
___Clpsed Structure ___Inter. Bld. ___Commercial   ___Industrial
___Lake   ___Pond   ___River   ___Creek
___From boat   ___From Shore

___ _____
___ _____
___ _____

Size of Search Area/Length of Trail:_____

Age of Exercise (i.e. hrs, days, etc):_____
Scent Article Used:_____**Age of Scent Article**:_____

Type of Exercise/Training:
___Agility   ___Directional   ___Obedience
___Socialization ___Area Search   ___Area Search w/ Pop-Up
___Runaway reps ___Trail   ___Area Search w/ Callout
___HRD   ___Water Recovery   ___Disaster   ___ Indication/Alert

Training Subjects:
___Location Known to handler   ___ Location Unknown to Handler
___Live/Mobile   ___Live/Immobile   ___Live/Concealed   ___Live/Bizarre

Behavior _____

Victim Description: ___Age   ___Race   ___Weight
                     ___Gender   ___Height   ___Other
HRD:
___HRD / Visible   ___HRD / Concealed   ___HRD / Overhead   ___HRD / Buried
HRD Sample Type/Age:
_____
_____

Sketch of Search Area and Exercise:

Comments: (Include evaluation of performance, plans for next training session, weaknesses, strengths.)

K9:_____ Handler:_____

Date:_____

Location:_____

Mileage: Beginning:_____ Ending:_____ Total:_____

Beginning Time: _____ Ending Time:_____ Total:_____

Conditions:

Wind Speed:_____ Wind Direction:_____ Humidity:_____ Temperature:_____

Cloud Cover:_____ Shadow (ft): _____ Other:_____

Rain:__ Hail:__ Snow:__ Sleet: __ Other:_____

Environment:

___Grass   ___Brush   ___Timber   ___Level
___Rolling   ___Steep   ___Thick   ___Thin
___Moderate   ___Rubble   ___Ext. Building   ___Residential
___Clpsed Structure ___Inter. Bld.   ___Commercial   ___Industrial
___Lake   ___Pond   ___River   ___Creek
___From boat   ___From Shore

___ _____
___ _____
___ _____

Size of Search Area/Length of Trail:_____

Age of Exercise (i.e. hrs, days, etc):_____

Scent Article Used:_____ **Age of Scent Article:**_____

Type of Exercise/Training:

___Agility   ___Directional   ___Obedience
___Socialization   ___Area Search   ___Area Search w/ Pop-Up
___Runaway reps   ___Trail   ___Area Search w/ Callout
___HRD   ___Water Recovery ___Disaster   ___ Indication/Alert

Training Subjects:

___Location Known to handler   ___ Location Unknown to Handler
___Live/Mobile   ___Live/Immobile   ___Live/Concealed   ___Live/Bizarre

Behavior _____

Victim Description: ___Age   ___Race   ___Weight
                     ___Gender   ___Height   ___Other

HRD:

___HRD / Visible   ___HRD / Concealed   ___HRD / Overhead   ___HRD / Buried

HRD Sample Type/Age:

_____
_____

Sketch of Search Area and Exercise:

Comments: (Include evaluation of performance, plans for next training session, weaknesses, strengths.)

K9:_____ Handler:_____
Date:_____ _____
Location:_____
Mileage: Beginning:_____ Ending:_____ Total:_____
Beginning Time: _____ Ending Time:_____ Total:_____

Conditions:
Wind Speed:_____ Wind Direction:_____ Humidity:_____ Temperature:_____
Cloud Cover:_____ Shadow (ft): _____ Other:_____
Rain:__ Hail:__ Snow:__ Sleet:__ Other:_____

Environment:
___Grass   ___Brush   ___Timber   ___Level
___Rolling   ___Steep   ___Thick   ___Thin
___Moderate   ___Rubble   ___Ext. Building ___Residential
___Clpsed Structure ___Inter. Bld. ___Commercial   ___Industrial
___Lake   ___Pond   ___River   ___Creek
___From boat   ___From Shore

___ _____
___ _____
___ _____

Size of Search Area/Length of Trail:_____

Age of Exercise (i.e. hrs, days, etc):_____
Scent Article Used:_____ **Age of Scent Article**:_____

Type of Exercise/Training:
___Agility   ___Directional   ___Obedience
___Socialization ___Area Search   ___Area Search w/ Pop-Up
___Runaway reps   ___Trail   ___Area Search w/ Callout
___HRD   ___Water Recovery ___Disaster   ___ Indication/Alert

Training Subjects:
___Location Known to handler   ___ Location Unknown to Handler
___Live/Mobile   ___Live/Immobile ___Live/Concealed ___Live/Bizarre

Behavior _____

Victim Description: ___Age   ___Race   ___Weight
                     ___Gender   ___Height   ___Other
HRD:
___HRD / Visible   ___HRD / Concealed ___HRD / Overhead ___HRD / Buried
HRD Sample Type/Age:
_____
_____

46

Sketch of Search Area and Exercise:

Comments: (Include evaluation of performance, plans for next training session, weaknesses, strengths.)

K9:_____ Handler:_____
Date:_____ _____
Location:_____
Mileage: Beginning:_____ Ending:_____ Total:_____
Beginning Time: _____ Ending Time:_____ Total:_____

Conditions:
Wind Speed:_____ Wind Direction:_____ Humidity:_____ Temperature:_____
Cloud Cover:_____ Shadow (ft): _____ Other:_____
Rain:__ Hail:__ Snow:__ Sleet:__ Other:_____

Environment:
___Grass   ___Brush   ___Timber   ___Level
___Rolling   ___Steep   ___Thick   ___Thin
___Moderate   ___Rubble   ___Ext. Building ___Residential
___Clpsed Structure ___Inter. Bld. ___Commercial   ___Industrial
___Lake   ___Pond   ___River   ___Creek
___From boat   ___From Shore

___ _____
___ _____
___ _____

Size of Search Area/Length of Trail:_____

Age of Exercise (i.e. hrs, days, etc):_____
Scent Article Used:_____ **Age of Scent Article**:_____

Type of Exercise/Training:
___Agility   ___Directional   ___Obedience
___Socialization ___Area Search   ___Area Search w/ Pop-Up
___Runaway reps ___Trail   ___Area Search w/ Callout
___HRD   ___Water Recovery ___Disaster   ___ Indication/Alert

Training Subjects:
___Location Known to handler   ___ Location Unknown to Handler
___Live/Mobile   ___Live/Immobile   ___Live/Concealed   ___Live/Bizarre

Behavior _____

Victim Description: ___Age   ___Race   ___Weight
                     ___Gender   ___Height   ___Other
HRD:
___HRD / Visible   ___HRD / Concealed   ___HRD / Overhead   ___HRD / Buried
HRD Sample Type/Age:
_____
_____

Sketch of Search Area and Exercise:

Comments: (Include evaluation of performance, plans for next training session, weaknesses, strengths.)

K9:_____ Handler:_____

Date:_____ _____

Location:_____

Mileage: Beginning:_____ Ending:_____ Total:_____

Beginning Time: _____ Ending Time:_____ Total:_____

Conditions:

Wind Speed:_____ Wind Direction:_____ Humidity:_____ Temperature:_____

Cloud Cover:_____ Shadow (ft): _____ Other:_____

Rain:__ Hail:__ Snow:__ Sleet: __ Other:_____

Environment:

___Grass	___Brush	___Timber	___Level
___Rolling	___Steep	___Thick	___Thin
___Moderate	___Rubble	___Ext. Building	___Residential
___Clpsed Structure	___Inter. Bld.	___Commercial	___Industrial
___Lake	___Pond	___River	___Creek
___From boat	___From Shore		

___ _____

___ _____

___ _____

Size of Search Area/Length of Trail:_____

Age of Exercise (i.e. hrs, days, etc):_____

Scent Article Used:_____ **Age of Scent Article**:_____

Type of Exercise/Training:

___Agility	___Directional	___Obedience
___Socialization	___Area Search	___Area Search w/ Pop-Up
___Runaway reps	___Trail	___Area Search w/ Callout
___HRD	___Water Recovery	___Disaster ___ Indication/Alert

Training Subjects:

___Location Known to handler   ___ Location Unknown to Handler

___Live/Mobile   ___Live/Immobile   ___Live/Concealed   ___Live/Bizarre

Behavior _____

Victim Description: ___Age   ___Race   ___Weight
                       ___Gender   ___Height   ___Other

HRD:

___HRD / Visible   ___HRD / Concealed   ___HRD / Overhead   ___HRD / Buried

HRD Sample Type/Age:

_____

_____

Sketch of Search Area and Exercise:

Comments: (Include evaluation of performance, plans for next training session, weaknesses, strengths.)

K9:_____ Handler:_____
Date:_____
Location:_____
Mileage: Beginning:_____Ending:_____ Total:_____
Beginning Time: _____Ending Time:_____ Total:_____

Conditions:
Wind Speed:_____ Wind Direction:_____ Humidity:_____ Temperature:_____
Cloud Cover:_____ Shadow (ft): _____ Other:_____
Rain:___ Hail:___ Snow:___ Sleet: ___ Other:_____

Environment:
___Grass ___Brush ___Timber ___Level
___Rolling ___Steep ___Thick ___Thin
___Moderate ___Rubble ___Ext. Building ___Residential
___Clpsed Structure ___Inter. Bld. ___Commercial ___Industrial
___Lake ___Pond ___River ___Creek
___From boat ___From Shore

___ _____
___ _____
___ _____

Size of Search Area/Length of Trail:_____

Age of Exercise (i.e. hrs, days, etc):_____
Scent Article Used:_____**Age of Scent Article**:_____

Type of Exercise/Training:
___Agility ___Directional ___Obedience
___Socialization ___Area Search ___Area Search w/ Pop-Up
___Runaway reps ___Trail ___Area Search w/ Callout
___HRD ___Water Recovery ___Disaster ___ Indication/Alert

Training Subjects:
___Location Known to handler ___ Location Unknown to Handler
___Live/Mobile ___Live/Immobile ___Live/Concealed ___Live/Bizarre

Behavior _____

Victim Description: ___Age ___Race ___Weight
 ___Gender ___ Height ___Other
HRD:
___HRD / Visible ___HRD / Concealed ___HRD / Overhead ___HRD / Buried
HRD Sample Type/Age:
_____
_____

Sketch of Search Area and Exercise:

Comments: (Include evaluation of performance, plans for next training session, weaknesses, strengths.)

K9:_____ Handler:_____
Date:_____   _____
Location:_____
Mileage: Beginning:_____ Ending:_____ Total:_____
Beginning Time: _____ Ending Time:_____ Total:_____

Conditions:
Wind Speed:_____ Wind Direction:_____ Humidity:_____ Temperature:_____
Cloud Cover:_____ Shadow (ft): _____ Other:_____
Rain:__ Hail:__ Snow:__ Sleet: __ Other:_____

Environment:
___Grass   ___Brush   ___Timber   ___Level
___Rolling   ___Steep   ___Thick   ___Thin
___Moderate   ___Rubble   ___Ext. Building   ___Residential
___Clpsed Structure ___Inter. Bld. ___Commercial   ___Industrial
___Lake   ___Pond   ___River   ___Creek
___From boat   ___From Shore

___ _____
___ _____
___ _____

Size of Search Area/Length of Trail:_____

Age of Exercise (i.e. hrs, days, etc):_____
Scent Article Used:_____ **Age of Scent Article**:_____

Type of Exercise/Training:
___Agility   ___Directional   ___Obedience
___Socialization ___Area Search   ___Area Search w/ Pop-Up
___Runaway reps   ___Trail   ___Area Search w/ Callout
___HRD   ___Water Recovery ___Disaster   ___ Indication/Alert

Training Subjects:
___Location Known to handler   ___ Location Unknown to Handler
___Live/Mobile   ___Live/Immobile   ___Live/Concealed   ___Live/Bizarre

Behavior _____

Victim Description: ___Age   ___Race   ___Weight
                      ___Gender   ___Height   ___Other
HRD:
___HRD / Visible   ___HRD / Concealed   ___HRD / Overhead   ___HRD / Buried
HRD Sample Type/Age:
_____
_____

Sketch of Search Area and Exercise:

Comments: (Include evaluation of performance, plans for next training session, weaknesses, strengths.)

K9:_____ Handler:_____

Date:_____ _____

Location:_____

Mileage: Beginning:_____ Ending:_____ Total:_____

Beginning Time: _____ Ending Time:_____ Total:_____

Conditions:

Wind Speed:_____ Wind Direction:_____ Humidity:_____ Temperature:_____

Cloud Cover:_____ Shadow (ft): _____ Other:_____

Rain:__ Hail:__ Snow:__ Sleet: __ Other:_____

Environment:

___Grass	___Brush	___Timber	___Level
___Rolling	___Steep	___Thick	___Thin
___Moderate	___Rubble	___Ext. Building	___Residential
___Clpsed Structure	___Inter. Bld.	___Commercial	___Industrial
___Lake	___Pond	___River	___Creek
___From boat	___From Shore		

___ _____
___ _____
___ _____

Size of Search Area/Length of Trail:_____

Age of Exercise (i.e. hrs, days, etc):_____

Scent Article Used:_____ **Age of Scent Article**:_____

Type of Exercise/Training:

___Agility	___Directional	___Obedience
___Socialization	___Area Search	___Area Search w/ Pop-Up
___Runaway reps	___Trail	___Area Search w/ Callout
___HRD	___Water Recovery	___Disaster ___ Indication/Alert

Training Subjects:

___Location Known to handler   ___ Location Unknown to Handler

___Live/Mobile   ___Live/Immobile   ___Live/Concealed   ___Live/Bizarre

Behavior _____

Victim Description: ___Age   ___Race   ___Weight
                     ___Gender   ___Height   ___Other

HRD:

___HRD / Visible   ___HRD / Concealed   ___HRD / Overhead   ___HRD / Buried

HRD Sample Type/Age:

_____
_____

Sketch of Search Area and Exercise:

Comments: (Include evaluation of performance, plans for next training session, weaknesses, strengths.)

K9:_____ Handler:_____
Date:_____
Location:_____
Mileage: Beginning:_____ Ending:_____ Total:_____
Beginning Time: _____ Ending Time:_____ Total:_____

Conditions:
Wind Speed:_____ Wind Direction:_____ Humidity:_____ Temperature:_____
Cloud Cover:_____ Shadow (ft): _____ Other:_____
Rain:___ Hail:___ Snow:___ Sleet: ___ Other:_____

Environment:
___Grass   ___Brush   ___Timber   ___Level
___Rolling   ___Steep   ___Thick   ___Thin
___Moderate   ___Rubble   ___Ext. Building ___Residential
___Clpsed Structure ___Inter. Bld. ___Commercial   ___Industrial
___Lake   ___Pond   ___River   ___Creek
___From boat   ___From Shore

___ _____
___ _____
___ _____

Size of Search Area/Length of Trail:_____

Age of Exercise (i.e. hrs, days, etc):_____
Scent Article Used:_____ **Age of Scent Article**:_____

Type of Exercise/Training:
___Agility   ___Directional   ___Obedience
___Socialization ___Area Search   ___Area Search w/ Pop-Up
___Runaway reps   ___Trail   ___Area Search w/ Callout
___HRD   ___Water Recovery ___Disaster   ___ Indication/Alert

Training Subjects:
___Location Known to handler   ___ Location Unknown to Handler
___Live/Mobile   ___Live/Immobile   ___Live/Concealed   ___Live/Bizarre

Behavior _____

Victim Description: ___Age   ___Race   ___Weight
                      ___Gender   ___ Height   ___Other
HRD:
___HRD / Visible   ___HRD / Concealed   ___HRD / Overhead   ___HRD / Buried
HRD Sample Type/Age:

_____
_____

Sketch of Search Area and Exercise:

Comments: (Include evaluation of performance, plans for next training session, weaknesses, strengths.)

K9:_____ Handler:_____
Date:_____
Location:_____
Mileage: Beginning:_____ Ending:_____ Total:_____
Beginning Time: _____ Ending Time:_____ Total:_____

Conditions:
Wind Speed:_____ Wind Direction:_____ Humidity:_____ Temperature:_____
Cloud Cover:_____ Shadow (ft): _____ Other:_____
Rain:__ Hail:__ Snow:__ Sleet: __ Other:_____

Environment:
___Grass ___Brush ___Timber ___Level
___Rolling ___Steep ___Thick ___Thin
___Moderate ___Rubble ___Ext. Building ___Residential
___Clpsed Structure ___Inter. Bld. ___Commercial ___Industrial
___Lake ___Pond ___River ___Creek
___From boat ___From Shore

___ _____
___ _____
___ _____

Size of Search Area/Length of Trail:_____

Age of Exercise (i.e. hrs, days, etc):_____
Scent Article Used:_____ **Age of Scent Article:**_____

Type of Exercise/Training:
___Agility ___Directional ___Obedience
___Socialization ___Area Search ___Area Search w/ Pop-Up
___Runaway reps ___Trail ___Area Search w/ Callout
___HRD ___Water Recovery ___Disaster ___ Indication/Alert

Training Subjects:
___Location Known to handler ___ Location Unknown to Handler
___Live/Mobile ___Live/Immobile ___Live/Concealed ___Live/Bizarre

Behavior _____

Victim Description: ___Age ___Race ___Weight
                     ___Gender ___Height ___Other

HRD:
___HRD / Visible ___HRD / Concealed ___HRD / Overhead ___HRD / Buried
HRD Sample Type/Age:

_____
_____

Sketch of Search Area and Exercise:

Comments: (Include evaluation of performance, plans for next training session, weaknesses, strengths.)

K9:_____ Handler:_____
Date:_____
Location:_____
Mileage: Beginning:_____ Ending:_____ Total:_____
Beginning Time: _____ Ending Time:_____ Total:_____

Conditions:
Wind Speed:_____ Wind Direction:_____ Humidity:_____ Temperature:_____
Cloud Cover:_____ Shadow (ft): _____ Other:_____
Rain:__ Hail:__ Snow:__ Sleet:__ Other:_____

Environment:
___Grass   ___Brush   ___Timber   ___Level
___Rolling   ___Steep   ___Thick   ___Thin
___Moderate   ___Rubble   ___Ext. Building ___Residential
___Clpsed Structure ___Inter. Bld. ___Commercial ___Industrial
___Lake   ___Pond   ___River   ___Creek
___From boat   ___From Shore

___ _____
___ _____
___ _____

Size of Search Area/Length of Trail:_____

Age of Exercise (i.e. hrs, days, etc):_____
Scent Article Used:_____ **Age of Scent Article**:_____

Type of Exercise/Training:
___Agility   ___Directional   ___Obedience
___Socialization ___Area Search   ___Area Search w/ Pop-Up
___Runaway reps   ___Trail   ___Area Search w/ Callout
___HRD   ___Water Recovery ___Disaster   ___ Indication/Alert

Training Subjects:
___Location Known to handler   ___ Location Unknown to Handler
___Live/Mobile   ___Live/Immobile ___Live/Concealed ___Live/Bizarre

Behavior _____

Victim Description: ___Age   ___Race   ___Weight
                     ___Gender   ___Height   ___Other
HRD:
___HRD / Visible   ___HRD / Concealed ___HRD / Overhead ___HRD / Buried
HRD Sample Type/Age:

_____
_____

Sketch of Search Area and Exercise:

Comments: (Include evaluation of performance, plans for next training session, weaknesses, strengths.)

K9:_____ Handler:_____
Date:_____
Location:_____
Mileage: Beginning:_____Ending:_____Total:_____
Beginning Time: _____Ending Time:_____ Total:_____

Conditions:
Wind Speed:_____ Wind Direction:_____ Humidity:_____ Temperature:_____
Cloud Cover:_____ Shadow (ft): _____ Other:_____
Rain:__   Hail:__   Snow:__ Sleet: __ Other:_____

Environment:
___Grass   ___Brush   ___Timber   ___Level
___Rolling   ___Steep   ___Thick   ___Thin
___Moderate   ___Rubble   ___Ext. Building   ___Residential
___Clpsed Structure ___Inter. Bld. ___Commercial   ___Industrial
___Lake   ___Pond   ___River   ___Creek
___From boat   ___From Shore
_____
_____
_____

Size of Search Area/Length of Trail:_____

Age of Exercise (i.e. hrs, days, etc):_____
Scent Article Used:_____**Age of Scent Article**:_____

Type of Exercise/Training:
___Agility   ___Directional   ___Obedience
___Socialization   ___Area Search   ___Area Search w/ Pop-Up
___Runaway reps   ___Trail   ___Area Search w/ Callout
___HRD   ___Water Recovery   ___Disaster   ___ Indication/Alert

Training Subjects:
___Location Known to handler   ___ Location Unknown to Handler
___Live/Mobile   ___Live/Immobile   ___Live/Concealed   ___Live/Bizarre

Behavior _____

Victim Description: ___Age   ___Race   ___Weight
                     ___Gender   ___Height   ___Other
HRD:
___HRD / Visible   ___HRD / Concealed ___HRD / Overhead ___HRD / Buried
HRD Sample Type/Age:
_____
_____

Sketch of Search Area and Exercise:

Comments: (Include evaluation of performance, plans for next training session, weaknesses, strengths.)

K9:_____ Handler:_____
Date:_____
Location:_____
Mileage: Beginning:_____Ending:_____Total:_____
Beginning Time: _____Ending Time:_____ Total:_____

Conditions:
Wind Speed:_____ Wind Direction:_____ Humidity:_____ Temperature:_____
Cloud Cover:_____ Shadow (ft): _____ Other:_____
Rain:__ Hail:__ Snow:__ Sleet: __ Other:_____

Environment:
___Grass   ___Brush   ___Timber   ___Level
___Rolling   ___Steep   ___Thick   ___Thin
___Moderate   ___Rubble   ___Ext. Building ___Residential
___Clpsed Structure   ___Inter. Bld.   ___Commercial   ___Industrial
___Lake   ___Pond   ___River   ___Creek
___From boat   ___From Shore

___ _____
___ _____
___ _____

Size of Search Area/Length of Trail:_____

Age of Exercise (i.e. hrs, days, etc):_____
Scent Article Used:_____**Age of Scent Article**:_____

Type of Exercise/Training:
___Agility   ___Directional   ___Obedience
___Socialization   ___Area Search   ___Area Search w/ Pop-Up
___Runaway reps   ___Trail   ___Area Search w/ Callout
___HRD   ___Water Recovery   ___Disaster   ___ Indication/Alert

Training Subjects:
___Location Known to handler   ___ Location Unknown to Handler
___Live/Mobile   ___Live/Immobile   ___Live/Concealed   ___Live/Bizarre

Behavior _____

Victim Description: ___Age   ____Race   ____Weight
                      ____Gender   ____Height   ____Other
HRD:
___HRD / Visible   ____HRD / Concealed____HRD / Overhead____HRD / Buried
HRD Sample Type/Age:

_____
_____

Sketch of Search Area and Exercise:

Comments: (Include evaluation of performance, plans for next training session, weaknesses, strengths.)

K9:_____ Handler:_____
Date:_____   _____
Location:_____
Mileage: Beginning:_____ Ending:_____ Total:_____
Beginning Time: _____ Ending Time:_____ Total:_____

Conditions:
Wind Speed:_____ Wind Direction:_____ Humidity:_____ Temperature:_____
Cloud Cover:_____ Shadow (ft): _____ Other:_____
Rain:__   Hail:__   Snow:__   Sleet: __   Other:_____

Environment:
___Grass   ___Brush   ___Timber   ___Level
___Rolling   ___Steep   ___Thick   ___Thin
___Moderate   ___Rubble   ___Ext. Building   ___Residential
___Clpsed Structure ___Inter. Bld.   ___Commercial   ___Industrial
___Lake   ___Pond   ___River   ___Creek
___From boat   ___From Shore

___ _____
___ _____
___ _____

Size of Search Area/Length of Trail:_____

Age of Exercise (i.e. hrs, days, etc):_____
Scent Article Used:_____**Age of Scent Article**:_____

Type of Exercise/Training:
___Agility   ___Directional   ___Obedience
___Socialization   ___Area Search   ___Area Search w/ Pop-Up
___Runaway reps   ___Trail   ___Area Search w/ Callout
___HRD   ___Water Recovery ___Disaster   ___ Indication/Alert

Training Subjects:
___Location Known to handler   ___ Location Unknown to Handler
___Live/Mobile   ___Live/Immobile   ___Live/Concealed   ___Live/Bizarre

Behavior _____

Victim Description: ___Age   ___Race   ___Weight
                      ___Gender   ___Height   ___Other
HRD:
___HRD / Visible   ___HRD / Concealed ___HRD / Overhead   ___HRD / Buried
HRD Sample Type/Age:
_____
_____

Sketch of Search Area and Exercise:

Comments: (Include evaluation of performance, plans for next training session, weaknesses, strengths.)

K9:_____ Handler:_____
Date:_____
Location:_____
Mileage: Beginning:_____Ending:_____Total:_____
Beginning Time: _____Ending Time:_____ Total:_____

Conditions:
Wind Speed:_____ Wind Direction:_____ Humidity:_____ Temperature:_____
Cloud Cover:_____ Shadow (ft): _____ Other:_____
Rain:___ Hail:___ Snow:___ Sleet: ___ Other:_____

Environment:
___Grass   ___Brush   ___Timber   ___Level
___Rolling   ___Steep   ___Thick   ___Thin
___Moderate   ___Rubble   ___Ext. Building   ___Residential
___Clpsed Structure ___Inter. Bld. ___Commercial   ___Industrial
___Lake   ___Pond   ___River   ___Creek
___From boat   ___From Shore

___ _____
___ _____
___ _____

Size of Search Area/Length of Trail:_____

Age of Exercise (i.e. hrs, days, etc):_____
Scent Article Used:_____**Age of Scent Article**:_____

Type of Exercise/Training:
___Agility   ___Directional   ___Obedience
___Socialization ___Area Search   ___Area Search w/ Pop-Up
___Runaway reps   ___Trail   ___Area Search w/ Callout
___HRD   ___Water Recovery ___Disaster   ___ Indication/Alert

Training Subjects:
___Location Known to handler   ___ Location Unknown to Handler
___Live/Mobile   ___Live/Immobile   ___Live/Concealed ___Live/Bizarre

Behavior _____

Victim Description: ___Age   ___Race   ___Weight
                     ___Gender   ___Height   ___Other
HRD:
___HRD / Visible   ___HRD / Concealed___HRD / Overhead___HRD / Buried
HRD Sample Type/Age:
_____
_____

Sketch of Search Area and Exercise:

Comments: (Include evaluation of performance, plans for next training session, weaknesses, strengths.)

K9:_____ Handler:_____
Date:_____ _____
Location:_____
Mileage: Beginning:_____Ending:_____Total:_____
Beginning Time: _____Ending Time:_____ Total:_____

Conditions:
Wind Speed:_____ Wind Direction:_____ Humidity:_____ Temperature:_____
Cloud Cover:_____ Shadow (ft): _____ Other:_____
Rain:__ Hail:__ Snow:__ Sleet: __ Other:_____

Environment:
___Grass   ___Brush   ___Timber   ___Level
___Rolling   ___Steep   ___Thick   ___Thin
___Moderate   ___Rubble   ___Ext. Building ___Residential
___Clpsed Structure ___Inter. Bld. ___Commercial   ___Industrial
___Lake   ___Pond   ___River   ___Creek
___From boat   ___From Shore

___ _____
___ _____
___ _____

Size of Search Area/Length of Trail:_____

Age of Exercise (i.e. hrs, days, etc):_____
Scent Article Used:_____**Age of Scent Article**:_____

Type of Exercise/Training:
___Agility   ___Directional   ___Obedience
___Socialization ___Area Search   ___Area Search w/ Pop-Up
___Runaway reps   ___Trail   ___Area Search w/ Callout
___HRD   ___Water Recovery ___Disaster   ___ Indication/Alert

Training Subjects:
___Location Known to handler   ___ Location Unknown to Handler
___Live/Mobile   ___Live/Immobile   ___Live/Concealed   ___Live/Bizarre

Behavior _____

Victim Description: ___Age   ___Race   ___Weight
                     ___Gender   ___Height   ___Other

HRD:
___HRD / Visible   ___HRD / Concealed   ___HRD / Overhead   ___HRD / Buried
HRD Sample Type/Age:
_____
_____

Sketch of Search Area and Exercise:

Comments: (Include evaluation of performance, plans for next training session, weaknesses, strengths.)

K9:_____ Handler:_____
Date:_____
Location:_____
Mileage: Beginning:_____ Ending:_____ Total:_____
Beginning Time: _____ Ending Time:_____ Total:_____

Conditions:
Wind Speed:_____ Wind Direction:_____ Humidity:_____ Temperature:_____
Cloud Cover:_____ Shadow (ft): _____ Other:_____
Rain:__ Hail:__ Snow:__ Sleet: __ Other:_____

Environment:
___Grass   ___Brush   ___Timber   ___Level
___Rolling   ___Steep   ___Thick   ___Thin
___Moderate   ___Rubble   ___Ext. Building ___Residential
___Clpsed Structure ___Inter. Bld. ___Commercial ___Industrial
___Lake   ___Pond   ___River   ___Creek
___From boat   ___From Shore

___ _____
___ _____
___ _____

Size of Search Area/Length of Trail:_____

Age of Exercise (i.e. hrs, days, etc):_____
Scent Article Used:_____ **Age of Scent Article**:_____

Type of Exercise/Training:
___Agility   ___Directional   ___Obedience
___Socialization ___Area Search   ___Area Search w/ Pop-Up
___Runaway reps ___Trail   ___Area Search w/ Callout
___HRD   ___Water Recovery ___Disaster   ___ Indication/Alert

Training Subjects:
___Location Known to handler   ___ Location Unknown to Handler
___Live/Mobile   ___Live/Immobile   ___Live/Concealed   ___Live/Bizarre

Behavior _____

Victim Description: ___Age   ___Race   ___Weight
                     ___Gender   ___Height   ___Other
HRD:
___HRD / Visible   ___HRD / Concealed   ___HRD / Overhead   ___HRD / Buried
HRD Sample Type/Age:
_____
_____

Sketch of Search Area and Exercise:

Comments: (Include evaluation of performance, plans for next training session, weaknesses, strengths.)

K9:_____ Handler:_____
Date:_____
Location:_____
Mileage: Beginning:_____ Ending:_____ Total:_____
Beginning Time: _____ Ending Time:_____ Total:_____

Conditions:
Wind Speed:_____ Wind Direction:_____ Humidity:_____ Temperature:_____
Cloud Cover:_____ Shadow (ft): _____ Other:_____
Rain:__ Hail:__ Snow:__ Sleet: __ Other:_____

Environment:
___Grass   ___Brush   ___Timber   ___Level
___Rolling   ___Steep   ___Thick   ___Thin
___Moderate   ___Rubble   ___Ext. Building   ___Residential
___Clpsed Structure ___Inter. Bld. ___Commercial   ___Industrial
___Lake   ___Pond   ___River   ___Creek
___From boat   ___From Shore

___ _____
___ _____
___ _____

Size of Search Area/Length of Trail:_____

Age of Exercise (i.e. hrs, days, etc):_____
Scent Article Used:_____**Age of Scent Article**:_____

Type of Exercise/Training:
___Agility   ___Directional   ___Obedience
___Socialization ___Area Search   ___Area Search w/ Pop-Up
___Runaway reps   ___Trail   ___Area Search w/ Callout
___HRD   ___Water Recovery ___Disaster   ___ Indication/Alert

Training Subjects:
___Location Known to handler   ___ Location Unknown to Handler
___Live/Mobile   ___Live/Immobile   ___Live/Concealed   ___Live/Bizarre

Behavior _____

Victim Description: ___Age   ___Race   ___Weight
                     ___Gender   ___Height   ___Other
HRD:
___HRD / Visible ___HRD / Concealed ___HRD / Overhead ___HRD / Buried
HRD Sample Type/Age:
_____
_____

Sketch of Search Area and Exercise:

Comments: (Include evaluation of performance, plans for next training session, weaknesses, strengths.)

K9:_____   Handler:_____
Date:_____   _____
Location:_____
Mileage: Beginning:_____ Ending:_____ Total:_____
Beginning Time: _____ Ending Time:_____ Total:_____

Conditions:
Wind Speed:_____ Wind Direction:_____ Humidity:_____ Temperature:_____
Cloud Cover:_____ Shadow (ft): _____ Other:_____
Rain:__ Hail:__ Snow:__ Sleet: __ Other:_____

Environment:
___Grass   ___Brush   ___Timber   ___Level
___Rolling   ___Steep   ___Thick   ___Thin
___Moderate   ___Rubble   ___Ext. Building ___Residential
___Clpsed Structure ___Inter. Bld. ___Commercial   ___Industrial
___Lake   ___Pond   ___River   ___Creek
___From boat   ___From Shore

___ _____
___ _____
___ _____

Size of Search Area/Length of Trail:_____

Age of Exercise (i.e. hrs, days, etc):_____
Scent Article Used:_____ **Age of Scent Article**:_____

Type of Exercise/Training:
___Agility   ___Directional   ___Obedience
___Socialization ___Area Search   ___Area Search w/ Pop-Up
___Runaway reps   ___Trail   ___Area Search w/ Callout
___HRD   ___Water Recovery   ___Disaster   ___ Indication/Alert

Training Subjects:
___Location Known to handler   ___ Location Unknown to Handler
___Live/Mobile   ___Live/Immobile   ___Live/Concealed   ___Live/Bizarre

Behavior _____

Victim Description: ____Age   ____Race   ____Weight
                     ____Gender   ____Height   ____Other
HRD:
___HRD / Visible   ___HRD / Concealed ___HRD / Overhead ___HRD / Buried
HRD Sample Type/Age:

_____
_____

Sketch of Search Area and Exercise:

Comments: (Include evaluation of performance, plans for next training session, weaknesses, strengths.)

K9:_____   Handler:_____
Date:_____   _____
Location:_____
Mileage: Beginning:_____Ending:_____Total:_____
Beginning Time: _____Ending Time:_____ Total:_____

Conditions:
Wind Speed:_____ Wind Direction:_____ Humidity:_____ Temperature:_____
Cloud Cover:_____ Shadow (ft): _____ Other:_____
Rain:__ Hail:__ Snow:__ Sleet: __ Other:_____

Environment:
___Grass   ___Brush   ___Timber   ___Level
___Rolling   ___Steep   ___Thick   ___Thin
___Moderate   ___Rubble   ___Ext. Building ___Residential
___Clpsed Structure ___Inter. Bld. ___Commercial ___Industrial
___Lake   ___Pond   ___River   ___Creek
___From boat   ___From Shore
___ _____
___ _____
___ _____

Size of Search Area/Length of Trail:_____

Age of Exercise (i.e. hrs, days, etc):_____
Scent Article Used:_____**Age of Scent Article**:_____

Type of Exercise/Training:
___Agility   ___Directional   ___Obedience
___Socialization ___Area Search   ___Area Search w/ Pop-Up
___Runaway reps ___Trail   ___Area Search w/ Callout
___HRD   ___Water Recovery ___Disaster   ___ Indication/Alert

Training Subjects:
___Location Known to handler   ___ Location Unknown to Handler
___Live/Mobile   ___Live/Immobile   ___Live/Concealed ___Live/Bizarre

Behavior _____

Victim Description: ____Age   ____Race   ____Weight
                     ____Gender   ____Height   ____Other
HRD:
___HRD / Visible   ___HRD / Concealed ___HRD / Overhead ___HRD / Buried
HRD Sample Type/Age:
_____
_____

Sketch of Search Area and Exercise:

Comments: (Include evaluation of performance, plans for next training session, weaknesses, strengths.)

K9:_____ Handler:_____
Date:_____ _____
Location:_____
Mileage: Beginning:_____ Ending:_____ Total:_____
Beginning Time: _____ Ending Time:_____ Total:_____

Conditions:
Wind Speed:_____ Wind Direction:_____ Humidity:_____ Temperature:_____
Cloud Cover:_____ Shadow (ft): _____ Other:_____
Rain:___ Hail:___ Snow:___ Sleet: ___ Other:_____

Environment:
___Grass ___Brush ___Timber ___Level
___Rolling ___Steep ___Thick ___Thin
___Moderate ___Rubble ___Ext. Building ___Residential
___Clpsed Structure ___Inter. Bld. ___Commercial ___Industrial
___Lake ___Pond ___River ___Creek
___From boat ___From Shore

___ _____
___ _____
___ _____

Size of Search Area/Length of Trail:_____

Age of Exercise (i.e. hrs, days, etc):_____
Scent Article Used:_____**Age of Scent Article**:_____

Type of Exercise/Training:
___Agility ___Directional ___Obedience
___Socialization ___Area Search ___Area Search w/ Pop-Up
___Runaway reps ___Trail ___Area Search w/ Callout
___HRD ___Water Recovery ___Disaster ___ Indication/Alert

Training Subjects:
___Location Known to handler ___ Location Unknown to Handler
___Live/Mobile ___Live/Immobile ___Live/Concealed ___Live/Bizarre

Behavior _____

Victim Description: ____Age ____Race ____Weight
____Gender ____Height ____Other
HRD:
___HRD / Visible ____HRD / Concealed____HRD / Overhead____HRD / Buried
HRD Sample Type/Age:

_____
_____

Sketch of Search Area and Exercise:

Comments: (Include evaluation of performance, plans for next training session, weaknesses, strengths.)

K9:_____ Handler:_____
Date:_____ _____
Location:_____
Mileage: Beginning:_____ Ending:_____ Total:_____
Beginning Time: _____ Ending Time:_____ Total:_____

Conditions:
Wind Speed:_____ Wind Direction:_____ Humidity:_____ Temperature:_____
Cloud Cover:_____ Shadow (ft): _____ Other:_____
Rain:__ Hail:__ Snow:__ Sleet: __ Other:_____

Environment:
___Grass   ___Brush   ___Timber   ___Level
___Rolling   ___Steep   ___Thick   ___Thin
___Moderate   ___Rubble   ___Ext. Building   ___Residential
___Clpsed Structure ___Inter. Bld.   ___Commercial   ___Industrial
___Lake   ___Pond   ___River   ___Creek
___From boat   ___From Shore

___ _____
___ _____
___ _____

Size of Search Area/Length of Trail:_____

Age of Exercise (i.e. hrs, days, etc):_____
Scent Article Used:_____ **Age of Scent Article**:_____

Type of Exercise/Training:
___Agility   ___Directional   ___Obedience
___Socialization   ___Area Search   ___Area Search w/ Pop-Up
___Runaway reps   ___Trail   ___Area Search w/ Callout
___HRD   ___Water Recovery ___Disaster   ___ Indication/Alert

Training Subjects:
___Location Known to handler   ___ Location Unknown to Handler
___Live/Mobile   ___Live/Immobile   ___Live/Concealed   ___Live/Bizarre

Behavior _____

Victim Description: ___Age   ___Race   ___Weight
                     ___Gender   ___ Height   ___Other

HRD:
___HRD / Visible   ___HRD / Concealed ___HRD / Overhead ___HRD / Buried
HRD Sample Type/Age:

_____
_____

Sketch of Search Area and Exercise:

Comments: (Include evaluation of performance, plans for next training session, weaknesses, strengths.)

K9:_____ Handler:_____
Date:_____ _____
Location:_____
Mileage: Beginning:_____ Ending:_____ Total:_____
Beginning Time: _____ Ending Time:_____ Total:_____

Conditions:
Wind Speed:_____ Wind Direction:_____ Humidity:_____ Temperature:_____
Cloud Cover:_____ Shadow (ft): _____ Other:_____
Rain:__ Hail:__ Snow:__ Sleet: __ Other:_____

Environment:
___Grass   ___Brush   ___Timber   ___Level
___Rolling   ___Steep   ___Thick   ___Thin
___Moderate   ___Rubble   ___Ext. Building   ___Residential
___Clpsed Structure ___Inter. Bld. ___Commercial   ___Industrial
___Lake   ___Pond   ___River   ___Creek
___From boat   ___From Shore
___ _____
___ _____
___ _____

Size of Search Area/Length of Trail:_____

Age of Exercise (i.e. hrs, days, etc):_____
Scent Article Used:_____ **Age of Scent Article**:_____

Type of Exercise/Training:
___Agility   ___Directional   ___Obedience
___Socialization ___Area Search   ___Area Search w/ Pop-Up
___Runaway reps   ___Trail   ___Area Search w/ Callout
___HRD   ___Water Recovery ___Disaster   ___ Indication/Alert

Training Subjects:
___Location Known to handler   ___ Location Unknown to Handler
___Live/Mobile   ___Live/Immobile ___Live/Concealed ___Live/Bizarre

Behavior _____

Victim Description: ____Age   _____Race   ____Weight
                     ____Gender   ____ Height   _____Other
HRD:
___HRD / Visible ___HRD / Concealed ___HRD / Overhead ___HRD / Buried
HRD Sample Type/Age:
_____
_____

Sketch of Search Area and Exercise:

Comments: (Include evaluation of performance, plans for next training session, weaknesses, strengths.)

K9:_____ Handler:_____
Date:_____   _____
Location:_____
Mileage: Beginning:_____ Ending:_____ Total:_____
Beginning Time: _____ Ending Time:_____ Total:_____

Conditions:
Wind Speed:_____ Wind Direction:_____ Humidity:_____ Temperature:_____
Cloud Cover:_____ Shadow (ft): _____ Other:_____
Rain:__ Hail:__ Snow:__ Sleet: __ Other:_____

Environment:
___Grass   ___Brush   ___Timber   ___Level
___Rolling   ___Steep   ___Thick   ___Thin
___Moderate   ___Rubble   ___Ext. Building   ___Residential
___Clpsed Structure ___Inter. Bld. ___Commercial   ___Industrial
___Lake   ___Pond   ___River   ___Creek
___From boat   ___From Shore

___ _____
___ _____
___ _____

Size of Search Area/Length of Trail:_____

Age of Exercise (i.e. hrs, days, etc):_____
Scent Article Used:_____**Age of Scent Article**:_____

Type of Exercise/Training:
___Agility   ___Directional   ___Obedience
___Socialization   ___Area Search   ___Area Search w/ Pop-Up
___Runaway reps   ___Trail   ___Area Search w/ Callout
___HRD   ___Water Recovery ___Disaster   ___ Indication/Alert

Training Subjects:
___Location Known to handler   ___ Location Unknown to Handler
___Live/Mobile   ___Live/Immobile   ___Live/Concealed   ___Live/Bizarre

Behavior _____

Victim Description: ____Age   ____Race   ____Weight
                     ____Gender   ____Height   ____Other
HRD:
___HRD / Visible   ___HRD / Concealed ___HRD / Overhead ___HRD / Buried
HRD Sample Type/Age:

_____
_____

Sketch of Search Area and Exercise:

Comments: (Include evaluation of performance, plans for next training session, weaknesses, strengths.)

K9:_____ Handler:_____
Date:_____ _____
Location:_____
Mileage: Beginning:_____Ending:_____ Total:_____
Beginning Time: _____Ending Time:_____ Total:_____

Conditions:
Wind Speed:_____ Wind Direction:_____ Humidity:_____ Temperature:_____
Cloud Cover:_____ Shadow (ft): _____ Other:_____
Rain:__ Hail:__ Snow:__ Sleet: __ Other:_____

Environment:
___Grass   ___Brush   ___Timber   ___Level
___Rolling   ___Steep   ___Thick   ___Thin
___Moderate   ___Rubble   ___Ext. Building ___Residential
___Clpsed Structure ___Inter. Bld. ___Commercial   ___Industrial
___Lake   ___Pond   ___River   ___Creek
___From boat   ___From Shore
___ _____
___ _____
___ _____

Size of Search Area/Length of Trail:_____

Age of Exercise (i.e. hrs, days, etc):_____
Scent Article Used:_____**Age of Scent Article**:_____

Type of Exercise/Training:
___Agility   ___Directional   ___Obedience
___Socialization ___Area Search   ___Area Search w/ Pop-Up
___Runaway reps ___Trail   ___Area Search w/ Callout
___HRD   ___Water Recovery ___Disaster   ___ Indication/Alert

Training Subjects:
___Location Known to handler   ___ Location Unknown to Handler
___Live/Mobile   ___Live/Immobile   ___Live/Concealed   ___Live/Bizarre

Behavior _____

Victim Description: ____Age   _____Race   _____Weight
                     ____Gender   ____ Height   _____Other
HRD:
___HRD / Visible   ___HRD / Concealed ___HRD / Overhead ___HRD / Buried
HRD Sample Type/Age:

_____
_____

Sketch of Search Area and Exercise:

Comments: (Include evaluation of performance, plans for next training session, weaknesses, strengths.)

K9:_____ Handler:_____
Date:_____ _____
Location:_____
Mileage: Beginning:_____ Ending:_____ Total:_____
Beginning Time: _____ Ending Time:_____ Total:_____

Conditions:
Wind Speed:_____ Wind Direction:_____ Humidity:_____ Temperature:_____
Cloud Cover:_____ Shadow (ft): _____ Other:_____
Rain:__ Hail:__ Snow:__ Sleet:__ Other:_____

Environment:
___Grass   ___Brush   ___Timber   ___Level
___Rolling   ___Steep   ___Thick   ___Thin
___Moderate   ___Rubble   ___Ext. Building ___Residential
___Clpsed Structure ___Inter. Bld. ___Commercial   ___Industrial
___Lake   ___Pond   ___River   ___Creek
___From boat   ___From Shore
___ _____
___ _____
___ _____

Size of Search Area/Length of Trail:_____

Age of Exercise (i.e. hrs, days, etc):_____
Scent Article Used:_____ **Age of Scent Article**:_____

Type of Exercise/Training:
___Agility   ___Directional   ___Obedience
___Socialization ___Area Search   ___Area Search w/ Pop-Up
___Runaway reps   ___Trail   ___Area Search w/ Callout
___HRD   ___Water Recovery ___Disaster   ___ Indication/Alert

Training Subjects:
___Location Known to handler   ___ Location Unknown to Handler
___Live/Mobile   ___Live/Immobile ___Live/Concealed ___Live/Bizarre

Behavior _____

Victim Description: ____Age   ____Race   ____Weight
                     ____Gender   ____Height   ____Other

HRD:
___HRD / Visible ___HRD / Concealed ___HRD / Overhead ___HRD / Buried
HRD Sample Type/Age:
_____
_____

Sketch of Search Area and Exercise:

Comments: (Include evaluation of performance, plans for next training session, weaknesses, strengths.)

K9:_____ Handler:_____
Date:_____ _____
Location:_____
Mileage: Beginning:_____Ending:_____ Total:_____
Beginning Time: _____ Ending Time:_____ Total:_____

Conditions:
Wind Speed:_____ Wind Direction:_____ Humidity:_____ Temperature:_____
Cloud Cover:_____ Shadow (ft): _____ Other:_____
Rain:__ Hail:__ Snow:__ Sleet: __ Other:_____

Environment:
___Grass   ___Brush   ___Timber   ___Level
___Rolling   ___Steep   ___Thick   ___Thin
___Moderate   ___Rubble   ___Ext. Building   ___Residential
___Clpsed Structure ___Inter. Bld. ___Commercial   ___Industrial
___Lake   ___Pond   ___River   ___Creek
___From boat   ___From Shore

___ _____
___ _____
___ _____

Size of Search Area/Length of Trail:_____

Age of Exercise (i.e. hrs, days, etc):_____
Scent Article Used:_____**Age of Scent Article**:_____

Type of Exercise/Training:
___Agility   ___Directional   ___Obedience
___Socialization   ___Area Search   ___Area Search w/ Pop-Up
___Runaway reps   ___Trail   ___Area Search w/ Callout
___HRD   ___Water Recovery   ___Disaster   ___ Indication/Alert

Training Subjects:
___Location Known to handler   ___ Location Unknown to Handler
___Live/Mobile   ___Live/Immobile   ___Live/Concealed   ___Live/Bizarre

Behavior _____

Victim Description: ____Age   ____Race   ____Weight
                     ____Gender   ____Height   ____Other

HRD:
___HRD / Visible   ___HRD / Concealed ___HRD / Overhead ___HRD / Buried
HRD Sample Type/Age:

_____
_____

Sketch of Search Area and Exercise:

Comments: (Include evaluation of performance, plans for next training session, weaknesses, strengths.)

K9:_____ Handler:_____
Date:_____ _____
Location:_____
Mileage: Beginning:_____ Ending:_____ Total:_____
Beginning Time: _____ Ending Time:_____ Total:_____

Conditions:
Wind Speed:_____ Wind Direction:_____ Humidity:_____ Temperature:_____
Cloud Cover:_____ Shadow (ft): _____ Other:_____
Rain:__ Hail:__ Snow:__ Sleet: __ Other:_____

Environment:
___Grass ___Brush ___Timber ___Level
___Rolling ___Steep ___Thick ___Thin
___Moderate ___Rubble ___Ext. Building ___Residential
___Clpsed Structure ___Inter. Bld. ___Commercial ___Industrial
___Lake ___Pond ___River ___Creek
___From boat ___From Shore

___ _____
___ _____
___ _____

Size of Search Area/Length of Trail:_____

Age of Exercise (i.e. hrs, days, etc):_____
Scent Article Used:_____ **Age of Scent Article**:_____

Type of Exercise/Training:
___Agility ___Directional ___Obedience
___Socialization ___Area Search ___Area Search w/ Pop-Up
___Runaway reps ___Trail ___Area Search w/ Callout
___HRD ___Water Recovery ___Disaster ___ Indication/Alert

Training Subjects:
___Location Known to handler ___ Location Unknown to Handler
___Live/Mobile ___Live/Immobile ___Live/Concealed ___Live/Bizarre

Behavior _____

Victim Description: ____Age ____Race ____Weight
 ____Gender ____Height ____Other
HRD:
___HRD / Visible ___HRD / Concealed ___HRD / Overhead ___HRD / Buried
HRD Sample Type/Age:

_____
_____

Sketch of Search Area and Exercise:

Comments: (Include evaluation of performance, plans for next training session, weaknesses, strengths.)

K9:_____ Handler:_____
Date:_____ _____
Location:_____
Mileage: Beginning:_____ Ending:_____ Total:_____
Beginning Time: _____ Ending Time:_____ Total:_____

Conditions:
Wind Speed:_____ Wind Direction:_____ Humidity:_____ Temperature:_____
Cloud Cover:_____ Shadow (ft): _____ Other:_____
Rain:__ Hail:__ Snow:__ Sleet: __ Other:_____

Environment:
___Grass   ___Brush   ___Timber   ___Level
___Rolling   ___Steep   ___Thick   ___Thin
___Moderate   ___Rubble   ___Ext. Building ___Residential
___Clpsed Structure ___Inter. Bld.   ___Commercial   ___Industrial
___Lake   ___Pond   ___River   ___Creek
___From boat   ___From Shore

___ _____
___ _____
___ _____

Size of Search Area/Length of Trail:_____

Age of Exercise (i.e. hrs, days, etc):_____
Scent Article Used:_____ **Age of Scent Article**:_____

Type of Exercise/Training:
___Agility   ___Directional   ___Obedience
___Socialization   ___Area Search   ___Area Search w/ Pop-Up
___Runaway reps   ___Trail   ___Area Search w/ Callout
___HRD   ___Water Recovery   ___Disaster   ___ Indication/Alert

Training Subjects:
___Location Known to handler   ___ Location Unknown to Handler
___Live/Mobile   ___Live/Immobile   ___Live/Concealed   ___Live/Bizarre

Behavior _____

Victim Description: ____Age   ____Race   ____Weight
                     ____Gender   ____Height   ____Other

HRD:
___HRD / Visible   ___HRD / Concealed   ___HRD / Overhead   ___HRD / Buried
HRD Sample Type/Age:

_____
_____

Sketch of Search Area and Exercise:

Comments: (Include evaluation of performance, plans for next training session, weaknesses, strengths.)

K9:_____ Handler:_____
Date:_____   _____
Location:_____
Mileage: Beginning:_____ Ending:_____ Total:_____
Beginning Time: _____ Ending Time:_____ Total:_____

Conditions:
Wind Speed:_____ Wind Direction:_____ Humidity:_____ Temperature:_____
Cloud Cover:_____ Shadow (ft): _____ Other:_____
Rain:___ Hail:___ Snow:___ Sleet: ___ Other:_____

Environment:
___Grass   ___Brush   ___Timber   ___Level
___Rolling   ___Steep   ___Thick   ___Thin
___Moderate   ___Rubble   ___Ext. Building ___Residential
___Clpsed Structure ___Inter. Bld. ___Commercial   ___Industrial
___Lake   ___Pond   ___River   ___Creek
___From boat   ___From Shore
___ _____
___ _____
___ _____

Size of Search Area/Length of Trail:_____

Age of Exercise (i.e. hrs, days, etc):_____
Scent Article Used:_____ **Age of Scent Article**:_____

Type of Exercise/Training:
___Agility   ___Directional   ___Obedience
___Socialization ___Area Search   ___Area Search w/ Pop-Up
___Runaway reps   ___Trail   ___Area Search w/ Callout
___HRD   ___Water Recovery ___Disaster   ___ Indication/Alert

Training Subjects:
___Location Known to handler   ___ Location Unknown to Handler
___Live/Mobile   ___Live/Immobile ___Live/Concealed ___Live/Bizarre

Behavior _____

Victim Description: ___Age   ___Race   ___Weight
                     ___Gender   ___Height   ___Other
HRD:
___HRD / Visible   ___HRD / Concealed   ___HRD / Overhead   ___HRD / Buried
HRD Sample Type/Age:
_____
_____

Sketch of Search Area and Exercise:

Comments: (Include evaluation of performance, plans for next training session, weaknesses, strengths.)

K9:_____ Handler:_____
Date:_____
Location:_____
Mileage: Beginning:_____ Ending:_____ Total:_____
Beginning Time: _____ Ending Time:_____ Total:_____

Conditions:
Wind Speed:_____ Wind Direction:_____ Humidity:_____ Temperature:_____
Cloud Cover:_____ Shadow (ft): _____ Other:_____
Rain:__ Hail:__ Snow:__ Sleet: __ Other:_____

Environment:
___Grass   ___Brush   ___Timber   ___Level
___Rolling   ___Steep   ___Thick   ___Thin
___Moderate   ___Rubble   ___Ext. Building ___Residential
___Clpsed Structure ___Inter. Bld. ___Commercial   ___Industrial
___Lake   ___Pond   ___River   ___Creek
___From boat   ___From Shore

___ _____
___ _____
___ _____

Size of Search Area/Length of Trail:_____

Age of Exercise (i.e. hrs, days, etc):_____
Scent Article Used:_____ **Age of Scent Article:**_____

Type of Exercise/Training:
___Agility   ___Directional   ___Obedience
___Socialization ___Area Search   ___Area Search w/ Pop-Up
___Runaway reps ___Trail   ___Area Search w/ Callout
___HRD   ___Water Recovery ___Disaster   ___ Indication/Alert

Training Subjects:
___Location Known to handler   ___ Location Unknown to Handler
___Live/Mobile   ___Live/Immobile   ___Live/Concealed   ___Live/Bizarre

Behavior _____

Victim Description: ____Age   ____Race   ____Weight
                     ____Gender   ____Height   ____Other

HRD:
___HRD / Visible ___HRD / Concealed ___HRD / Overhead ___HRD / Buried
HRD Sample Type/Age:

_____
_____

Sketch of Search Area and Exercise:

Comments: (Include evaluation of performance, plans for next training session, weaknesses, strengths.)

K9:_____ Handler:_____
Date:_____
_____
Location:_____
Mileage: Beginning:_____ Ending:_____ Total:_____
Beginning Time: _____ Ending Time:_____ Total:_____

Conditions:
Wind Speed:_____ Wind Direction:_____ Humidity:_____ Temperature:_____
Cloud Cover:_____ Shadow (ft): _____ Other:_____
Rain:__ Hail:__ Snow:__ Sleet: __ Other:_____

Environment:
___Grass   ___Brush   ___Timber   ___Level
___Rolling   ___Steep   ___Thick   ___Thin
___Moderate   ___Rubble   ___Ext. Building ___Residential
___Clpsed Structure ___Inter. Bld. ___Commercial   ___Industrial
___Lake   ___Pond   ___River   ___Creek
___From boat   ___From Shore
___ _____
___ _____
___ _____

Size of Search Area/Length of Trail:_____

Age of Exercise (i.e. hrs, days, etc):_____
Scent Article Used:_____ **Age of Scent Article**:_____

Type of Exercise/Training:
___Agility   ___Directional   ___Obedience
___Socialization ___Area Search   ___Area Search w/ Pop-Up
___Runaway reps ___Trail   ___Area Search w/ Callout
___HRD   ___Water Recovery ___Disaster   ___ Indication/Alert

Training Subjects:
___Location Known to handler   ___ Location Unknown to Handler
___Live/Mobile   ___Live/Immobile   ___Live/Concealed   ___Live/Bizarre

Behavior _____

Victim Description: ____Age   ____Race   ____Weight
                     ____Gender   ____Height   ____Other
HRD:
___HRD / Visible ___HRD / Concealed ___HRD / Overhead ___HRD / Buried
HRD Sample Type/Age:
_____
_____

104

Sketch of Search Area and Exercise:

Comments: (Include evaluation of performance, plans for next training session, weaknesses, strengths.)

K9:_____ Handler:_____
Date:_____   _____
Location:_____
Mileage: Beginning:_____Ending:_____ Total:_____
Beginning Time: _____Ending Time:_____ Total:_____

Conditions:
Wind Speed:_____ Wind Direction:_____ Humidity:_____ Temperature:_____
Cloud Cover:_____ Shadow (ft): _____ Other:_____
Rain:__ Hail:__ Snow:__ Sleet:__ Other:_____

Environment:
___Grass   ___Brush   ___Timber   ___Level
___Rolling   ___Steep   ___Thick   ___Thin
___Moderate   ___Rubble   ___Ext. Building ___Residential
___Clpsed Structure ___Inter. Bld. ___Commercial   ___Industrial
___Lake   ___Pond   ___River   ___Creek
___From boat   ___From Shore

___ _____
___ _____
___ _____

Size of Search Area/Length of Trail:_____

Age of Exercise (i.e. hrs, days, etc):_____
Scent Article Used:_____**Age of Scent Article**:_____

Type of Exercise/Training:
___Agility   ___Directional   ___Obedience
___Socialization ___Area Search   ___Area Search w/ Pop-Up
___Runaway reps ___Trail   ___Area Search w/ Callout
___HRD   ___Water Recovery ___Disaster   ___ Indication/Alert

Training Subjects:
___Location Known to handler   ___ Location Unknown to Handler
___Live/Mobile   ___Live/Immobile   ___Live/Concealed   ___Live/Bizarre

Behavior _____

Victim Description: ____Age   ____Race   ____Weight
                    ____Gender   ____Height   ____Other
HRD:
___HRD / Visible   ___HRD / Concealed ___HRD / Overhead ___HRD / Buried
HRD Sample Type/Age:

_____
_____

Sketch of Search Area and Exercise:

Comments: (Include evaluation of performance, plans for next training session, weaknesses, strengths.)

K9:_____ Handler:_____
Date:_____ _____
Location:_____
Mileage: Beginning:_____ Ending:_____ Total:_____
Beginning Time: _____ Ending Time:_____ Total:_____

Conditions:
Wind Speed:_____ Wind Direction:_____ Humidity:_____ Temperature:_____
Cloud Cover:_____ Shadow (ft): _____ Other:_____
Rain:__ Hail:__ Snow:__ Sleet:__ Other:_____

Environment:
___Grass   ___Brush   ___Timber   ___Level
___Rolling   ___Steep   ___Thick   ___Thin
___Moderate   ___Rubble   ___Ext. Building ___Residential
___Clpsed Structure ___Inter. Bld. ___Commercial   ___Industrial
___Lake   ___Pond   ___River   ___Creek
___From boat   ___From Shore
___ _____
___ _____
___ _____

Size of Search Area/Length of Trail:_____

Age of Exercise (i.e. hrs, days, etc):_____
Scent Article Used:_____ **Age of Scent Article**:_____

Type of Exercise/Training:
___Agility   ___Directional   ___Obedience
___Socialization ___Area Search   ___Area Search w/ Pop-Up
___Runaway reps   ___Trail   ___Area Search w/ Callout
___HRD   ___Water Recovery ___Disaster   ___ Indication/Alert

Training Subjects:
___Location Known to handler   ___ Location Unknown to Handler
___Live/Mobile   ___Live/Immobile   ___Live/Concealed   ___Live/Bizarre

Behavior _____

Victim Description: ____Age   ____Race   ____Weight
                     ____Gender   ____Height   ____Other

HRD:
___HRD / Visible   ___HRD / Concealed   ___HRD / Overhead   ___HRD / Buried
HRD Sample Type/Age:

_____
_____

Sketch of Search Area and Exercise:

Comments: (Include evaluation of performance, plans for next training session, weaknesses, strengths.)

K9:_____   Handler:_____
Date:_____   _____
Location:_____
Mileage: Beginning:_____Ending:_____ Total:_____
Beginning Time: _____Ending Time:_____ Total:_____

Conditions:
Wind Speed:_____ Wind Direction:_____ Humidity:_____ Temperature:_____
Cloud Cover:_____ Shadow (ft): _____ Other:_____
Rain:__ Hail:__ Snow:__ Sleet: __ Other:_____

Environment:
___Grass   ___Brush   ___Timber   ___Level
___Rolling   ___Steep   ___Thick   ___Thin
___Moderate   ___Rubble   ___Ext. Building ___Residential
___Clpsed Structure ___Inter. Bld. ___Commercial ___Industrial
___Lake   ___Pond   ___River   ___Creek
___From boat   ___From Shore
___ _____
___ _____
___ _____

Size of Search Area/Length of Trail:_____

Age of Exercise (i.e. hrs, days, etc):_____
Scent Article Used:_____ **Age of Scent Article**:_____

Type of Exercise/Training:
___Agility   ___Directional   ___Obedience
___Socialization ___Area Search   ___Area Search w/ Pop-Up
___Runaway reps ___Trail   ___Area Search w/ Callout
___HRD   ___Water Recovery ___Disaster   ___ Indication/Alert

Training Subjects:
___Location Known to handler   ___ Location Unknown to Handler
___Live/Mobile   ___Live/Immobile   ___Live/Concealed   ___Live/Bizarre

Behavior _____

Victim Description: ____Age   ____Race   ____Weight
                     ____Gender   ____Height   ____Other

HRD:
___HRD / Visible   ___HRD / Concealed   ___HRD / Overhead   ___HRD / Buried
HRD Sample Type/Age:

_____
_____

Sketch of Search Area and Exercise:

Comments: (Include evaluation of performance, plans for next training session, weaknesses, strengths.)

K9:_____ Handler:_____
Date:_____ _____
Location:_____
Mileage: Beginning:_____Ending:_____ Total:_____
Beginning Time: _____Ending Time:_____ Total:_____

Conditions:
Wind Speed:_____ Wind Direction:_____ Humidity:_____ Temperature:_____
Cloud Cover:_____ Shadow (ft): _____ Other:_____
Rain:__ Hail:__ Snow:__ Sleet: __ Other:_____

Environment:
___Grass ___Brush ___Timber ___Level
___Rolling ___Steep ___Thick ___Thin
___Moderate ___Rubble ___Ext. Building ___Residential
___Clpsed Structure ___Inter. Bld. ___Commercial ___Industrial
___Lake ___Pond ___River ___Creek
___From boat ___From Shore

___ _____
___ _____
___ _____

Size of Search Area/Length of Trail:_____

Age of Exercise (i.e. hrs, days, etc):_____
Scent Article Used:_____**Age of Scent Article**:_____

Type of Exercise/Training:
___Agility ___Directional ___Obedience
___Socialization ___Area Search ___Area Search w/ Pop-Up
___Runaway reps ___Trail ___Area Search w/ Callout
___HRD ___Water Recovery ___Disaster ___ Indication/Alert

Training Subjects:
___Location Known to handler ___ Location Unknown to Handler
___Live/Mobile ___Live/Immobile ___Live/Concealed ___Live/Bizarre

Behavior _____

Victim Description: ____Age ____Race ____Weight
                    ____Gender ____Height ____Other

HRD:
___HRD / Visible ____HRD / Concealed____HRD / Overhead_____HRD / Buried
HRD Sample Type/Age:

_____
_____

Sketch of Search Area and Exercise:

Comments: (Include evaluation of performance, plans for next training session, weaknesses, strengths.)

K9:_____ Handler:_____
Date:_____ _____
Location:_____
Mileage: Beginning:_____ Ending:_____ Total:_____
Beginning Time: _____ Ending Time:_____ Total:_____

Conditions:
Wind Speed:_____ Wind Direction:_____ Humidity:_____ Temperature:_____
Cloud Cover:_____ Shadow (ft): _____ Other:_____
Rain:___ Hail:___ Snow:___ Sleet:___ Other:_____

Environment:
___Grass   ___Brush   ___Timber   ___Level
___Rolling   ___Steep   ___Thick   ___Thin
___Moderate   ___Rubble   ___Ext. Building   ___Residential
___Clpsed Structure   ___Inter. Bld.   ___Commercial   ___Industrial
___Lake   ___Pond   ___River   ___Creek
___From boat   ___From Shore
___ _____
___ _____
___ _____

Size of Search Area/Length of Trail:_____

Age of Exercise (i.e. hrs, days, etc):_____
Scent Article Used:_____**Age of Scent Article**:_____

Type of Exercise/Training:
___Agility   ___Directional   ___Obedience
___Socialization   ___Area Search   ___Area Search w/ Pop-Up
___Runaway reps   ___Trail   ___Area Search w/ Callout
___HRD   ___Water Recovery ___Disaster   ___ Indication/Alert

Training Subjects:
___Location Known to handler   ___ Location Unknown to Handler
___Live/Mobile   ___Live/Immobile   ___Live/Concealed   ___Live/Bizarre

Behavior _____

Victim Description: ____Age   ____Race   ____Weight
                     ____Gender   ____Height   ____Other
HRD:
___HRD / Visible   ___HRD / Concealed ___HRD / Overhead ___HRD / Buried
HRD Sample Type/Age:
_____
_____

Sketch of Search Area and Exercise:

Comments: (Include evaluation of performance, plans for next training session, weaknesses, strengths.)

K9:_____ Handler:_____
Date:_____
Location:_____
Mileage: Beginning:_____ Ending:_____ Total:_____
Beginning Time: _____ Ending Time:_____ Total:_____

Conditions:
Wind Speed:_____ Wind Direction:_____ Humidity:_____ Temperature:_____
Cloud Cover:_____ Shadow (ft): _____ Other:_____
Rain:__ Hail:__ Snow:__ Sleet: __ Other:_____

Environment:
___Grass   ___Brush   ___Timber   ___Level
___Rolling   ___Steep   ___Thick   ___Thin
___Moderate   ___Rubble   ___Ext. Building ___Residential
___Clpsed Structure ___Inter. Bld. ___Commercial   ___Industrial
___Lake   ___Pond   ___River   ___Creek
___From boat   ___From Shore

___ _____
___ _____
___ _____

Size of Search Area/Length of Trail:_____

Age of Exercise (i.e. hrs, days, etc):_____
Scent Article Used:_____**Age of Scent Article**:_____

Type of Exercise/Training:
___Agility   ___Directional   ___Obedience
___Socialization ___Area Search   ___Area Search w/ Pop-Up
___Runaway reps   ___Trail   ___Area Search w/ Callout
___HRD   ___Water Recovery ___Disaster   ___ Indication/Alert

Training Subjects:
___Location Known to handler   ___ Location Unknown to Handler
___Live/Mobile   ___Live/Immobile   ___Live/Concealed   ___Live/Bizarre

Behavior _____

Victim Description: ____Age   _____Race   _____Weight
                     ____Gender   ____ Height   _____Other
HRD:
___HRD / Visible   ___HRD / Concealed ___HRD / Overhead ___HRD / Buried
HRD Sample Type/Age:
_____
_____

Sketch of Search Area and Exercise:

Comments: (Include evaluation of performance, plans for next training session, weaknesses, strengths.)

K9:_____ Handler:_____
Date:_____ _____
Location:_____
Mileage: Beginning:_____ Ending:_____ Total:_____
Beginning Time: _____ Ending Time:_____ Total:_____

Conditions:
Wind Speed:_____ Wind Direction:_____ Humidity:_____ Temperature:_____
Cloud Cover:_____ Shadow (ft): _____ Other:_____
Rain:__ Hail:__ Snow:__ Sleet: __ Other:_____

Environment:
___Grass ___Brush ___Timber ___Level
___Rolling ___Steep ___Thick ___Thin
___Moderate ___Rubble ___Ext. Building ___Residential
___Clpsed Structure ___Inter. Bld. ___Commercial ___Industrial
___Lake ___Pond ___River ___Creek
___From boat ___From Shore

___ _____
___ _____
___ _____

Size of Search Area/Length of Trail:_____

Age of Exercise (i.e. hrs, days, etc):_____
Scent Article Used:_____ **Age of Scent Article**:_____

Type of Exercise/Training:
___Agility ___Directional ___Obedience
___Socialization ___Area Search ___Area Search w/ Pop-Up
___Runaway reps ___Trail ___Area Search w/ Callout
___HRD ___Water Recovery ___Disaster ___ Indication/Alert

Training Subjects:
___Location Known to handler ___ Location Unknown to Handler
___Live/Mobile ___Live/Immobile ___Live/Concealed ___Live/Bizarre

Behavior _____

Victim Description: ___Age ___Race ___Weight
___Gender ___Height ___Other
HRD:
___HRD / Visible ___HRD / Concealed ___HRD / Overhead ___HRD / Buried
HRD Sample Type/Age:

_____
_____

Sketch of Search Area and Exercise:

Comments: (Include evaluation of performance, plans for next training session, weaknesses, strengths.)

K9:_____ Handler:_____
Date:_____   _____
Location:_____
Mileage: Beginning:_____ Ending:_____ Total:_____
Beginning Time: _____ Ending Time:_____ Total:_____

Conditions:
Wind Speed:_____ Wind Direction:_____ Humidity:_____ Temperature:_____
Cloud Cover:_____ Shadow (ft): _____ Other:_____
Rain:___ Hail:___ Snow:___ Sleet:___ Other:_____

Environment:
___Grass   ___Brush   ___Timber   ___Level
___Rolling   ___Steep   ___Thick   ___Thin
___Moderate   ___Rubble   ___Ext. Building   ___Residential
___Clpsed Structure ___Inter. Bld.   ___Commercial   ___Industrial
___Lake   ___Pond   ___River   ___Creek
___From boat   ___From Shore

___ _____
___ _____
___ _____

Size of Search Area/Length of Trail:_____

Age of Exercise (i.e. hrs, days, etc):_____
Scent Article Used:_____**Age of Scent Article**:_____

Type of Exercise/Training:
___Agility   ___Directional   ___Obedience
___Socialization   ___Area Search   ___Area Search w/ Pop-Up
___Runaway reps   ___Trail   ___Area Search w/ Callout
___HRD   ___Water Recovery ___Disaster   ___ Indication/Alert

Training Subjects:
___Location Known to handler   ___ Location Unknown to Handler
___Live/Mobile   ___Live/Immobile   ___Live/Concealed ___Live/Bizarre

Behavior _____

Victim Description: ____Age   _____Race   _____Weight
                     ____Gender   ____ Height   ____Other

HRD:
___HRD / Visible   ____HRD / Concealed ____HRD / Overhead ____HRD / Buried
HRD Sample Type/Age:

_____
_____

Sketch of Search Area and Exercise:

Comments: (Include evaluation of performance, plans for next training session, weaknesses, strengths.)

K9:_____   Handler:_____
Date:_____   _____
Location:_____
Mileage: Beginning:_____ Ending:_____   Total:_____
Beginning Time: _____ Ending Time:_____   Total:_____

Conditions:
Wind Speed:_____ Wind Direction:_____ Humidity:_____ Temperature:_____
Cloud Cover:_____ Shadow (ft): _____ Other:_____
Rain:__   Hail:__   Snow:__   Sleet: __   Other:_____

Environment:
___Grass   ___Brush   ___Timber   ___Level
___Rolling   ___Steep   ___Thick   ___Thin
___Moderate   ___Rubble   ___Ext. Building   ___Residential
___Clpsed Structure ___Inter. Bld. ___Commercial   ___Industrial
___Lake   ___Pond   ___River   ___Creek
___From boat   ___From Shore

___ _____
___ _____
___ _____

Size of Search Area/Length of Trail:_____

Age of Exercise (i.e. hrs, days, etc):_____
Scent Article Used:_____**Age of Scent Article**:_____

Type of Exercise/Training:
___Agility   ___Directional   ___Obedience
___Socialization   ___Area Search   ___Area Search w/ Pop-Up
___Runaway reps   ___Trail   ___Area Search w/ Callout
___HRD   ___Water Recovery   ___Disaster   ___ Indication/Alert

Training Subjects:
___Location Known to handler   ___ Location Unknown to Handler
___Live/Mobile   ___Live/Immobile   ___Live/Concealed   ___Live/Bizarre

Behavior _____

Victim Description: ____Age   _____Race   ____Weight
                     ____Gender   ____ Height   _____Other
HRD:
___HRD / Visible   ___HRD / Concealed   ___HRD / Overhead   ___HRD / Buried
HRD Sample Type/Age:

_____
_____

Sketch of Search Area and Exercise:

Comments: (Include evaluation of performance, plans for next training session, weaknesses, strengths.)

K9:_____   Handler:_____

Date:_____   _____

Location:_____

Mileage: Beginning:_____Ending:_____ Total:_____

Beginning Time: _____Ending Time:_____ Total:_____

Conditions:
Wind Speed:_____ Wind Direction:_____ Humidity:_____ Temperature:_____
Cloud Cover:_____ Shadow (ft): _____ Other:_____
Rain:__ Hail:__ Snow:__ Sleet: __ Other:_____

Environment:
___Grass   ___Brush   ___Timber   ___Level
___Rolling   ___Steep   ___Thick   ___Thin
___Moderate   ___Rubble   ___Ext. Building   ___Residential
___Clpsed Structure ___Inter. Bld. ___Commercial   ___Industrial
___Lake   ___Pond   ___River   ___Creek
___From boat   ___From Shore

___ _____
     _____
___ _____

Size of Search Area/Length of Trail:_____

Age of Exercise (i.e. hrs, days, etc):_____
Scent Article Used:_____**Age of Scent Article**:_____

Type of Exercise/Training:
___Agility   ___Directional   ___Obedience
___Socialization ___Area Search   ___Area Search w/ Pop-Up
___Runaway reps   ___Trail   ___Area Search w/ Callout
___HRD   ___Water Recovery ___Disaster   ___ Indication/Alert

Training Subjects:
___Location Known to handler   ___ Location Unknown to Handler
___Live/Mobile   ___Live/Immobile ___Live/Concealed ___Live/Bizarre

Behavior _____

Victim Description: ____Age   ____Race   ____Weight
                     ____Gender   ____ Height   ____Other

HRD:
___HRD / Visible   ___HRD / Concealed ___HRD / Overhead ___HRD / Buried
HRD Sample Type/Age:

_____
_____

Sketch of Search Area and Exercise:

Comments: (Include evaluation of performance, plans for next training session, weaknesses, strengths.)

K9:_____   Handler:_____
Date:_____   _____
Location:_____
Mileage: Beginning:_____ Ending:_____   Total:_____
Beginning Time: _____ Ending Time:_____   Total:_____

Conditions:
Wind Speed:_____ Wind Direction:_____ Humidity:_____ Temperature:_____
Cloud Cover:_____ Shadow (ft): _____ Other:_____
Rain:__ Hail:__ Snow:__ Sleet: __ Other:_____

Environment:
___Grass   ___Brush   ___Timber   ___Level
___Rolling   ___Steep   ___Thick   ___Thin
___Moderate   ___Rubble   ___Ext. Building ___Residential
___Clpsed Structure ___Inter. Bld.   ___Commercial   ___Industrial
___Lake   ___Pond   ___River   ___Creek
___From boat   ___From Shore

___ _____
___ _____
___ _____

Size of Search Area/Length of Trail:_____

Age of Exercise (i.e. hrs, days, etc):_____
Scent Article Used:_____ **Age of Scent Article**:_____

Type of Exercise/Training:
___Agility   ___Directional   ___Obedience
___Socialization   ___Area Search   ___Area Search w/ Pop-Up
___Runaway reps   ___Trail   ___Area Search w/ Callout
___HRD   ___Water Recovery   ___Disaster   ___ Indication/Alert

Training Subjects:
___Location Known to handler   ___ Location Unknown to Handler
___Live/Mobile   ___Live/Immobile   ___Live/Concealed   ___Live/Bizarre

Behavior _____

Victim Description: ____Age   ____Race   ____Weight
                     ____Gender   ____Height   ____Other
HRD:
___HRD / Visible   ___HRD / Concealed ___HRD / Overhead   ___HRD / Buried
HRD Sample Type/Age:
_____
_____

Sketch of Search Area and Exercise:

Comments: (Include evaluation of performance, plans for next training session, weaknesses, strengths.)

K9:_____ Handler:_____
Date:_____ _____
Location:_____
Mileage: Beginning:_____Ending:_____Total:_____
Beginning Time: _____Ending Time:_____Total:_____

Conditions:
Wind Speed:_____ Wind Direction:_____ Humidity:_____ Temperature:_____
Cloud Cover:_____ Shadow (ft): _____ Other:_____
Rain:__ Hail:__ Snow:__ Sleet: __ Other:_____

Environment:
___Grass ___Brush ___Timber ___Level
___Rolling ___Steep ___Thick ___Thin
___Moderate ___Rubble ___Ext. Building ___Residential
___Clpsed Structure ___Inter. Bld. ___Commercial ___Industrial
___Lake ___Pond ___River ___Creek
___From boat ___From Shore

___ _____
___ _____
___ _____

Size of Search Area/Length of Trail:_____

Age of Exercise (i.e. hrs, days, etc):_____
Scent Article Used:_____**Age of Scent Article**:_____

Type of Exercise/Training:
___Agility ___Directional ___Obedience
___Socialization ___Area Search ___Area Search w/ Pop-Up
___Runaway reps ___Trail ___Area Search w/ Callout
___HRD ___Water Recovery ___Disaster ___ Indication/Alert

Training Subjects:
___Location Known to handler ___ Location Unknown to Handler
___Live/Mobile ___Live/Immobile ___Live/Concealed ___Live/Bizarre

Behavior _____

Victim Description: ____Age ____Race ____Weight
 ____Gender ____Height ____Other
HRD:
___HRD / Visible ____HRD / Concealed____HRD / Overhead____HRD / Buried
HRD Sample Type/Age:
_____
_____

Sketch of Search Area and Exercise:

Comments: (Include evaluation of performance, plans for next training session, weaknesses, strengths.)

Section Five - SAR Mission Log

A. Log Summary

Date	Location	Requesting Agency	Missing Person (s)

Date	Location	Requesting Agency	Missing Person (s)

B. Mission Summaries

Date:_____ Location:_____

_____
_____
_____
_____
_____
_____
_____
_____
_____
_____

Date:_____ Location:_____

_____
_____
_____
_____
_____
_____
_____
_____
_____
_____

Date:_____ Location:_____

_____
_____
_____
_____
_____
_____
_____
_____
_____
_____

Date:_____ Location:_____

_____
_____
_____
_____
_____
_____
_____
_____
_____
_____

Date:_____ Location:_____

_____
_____
_____
_____
_____
_____
_____
_____
_____
_____

Date:_____ Location:_____

_____
_____
_____
_____
_____
_____
_____
_____
_____
_____

Date:_____ Location:_____

_____
_____
_____
_____
_____
_____
_____
_____
_____
_____

Date:_____ Location:_____

_____
_____
_____
_____
_____
_____
_____
_____
_____
_____

Date:_____ Location:_____

_____
_____
_____
_____
_____
_____
_____
_____
_____
_____

Date:_____ Location:_____

_____
_____
_____
_____
_____
_____
_____
_____
_____
_____

Date:_____ Location:_____

_____
_____
_____
_____
_____
_____
_____
_____
_____
_____

Date:_____ Location:_____

_____
_____
_____
_____
_____
_____
_____
_____
_____
_____

Date:_____ Location:_____

_____
_____
_____
_____
_____
_____
_____
_____
_____
_____

Date:_____ Location:_____

_____
_____
_____
_____
_____
_____
_____
_____
_____
_____

Date:_____ Location:_____

_____
_____
_____
_____
_____
_____
_____
_____
_____
_____

Date:_____ Location:_____

_____
_____
_____
_____
_____
_____
_____
_____
_____
_____

Date:_____ Location:_____

Date:_____ Location:_____

Date:_____ Location:_____

Date:_____ Location:_____

Date:_____ Location:_____
_____
_____
_____
_____
_____
_____
_____
_____
_____

Date:_____ Location:_____
_____
_____
_____
_____
_____
_____
_____
_____
_____

Date:_____ Location:_____
_____
_____
_____
_____
_____
_____
_____
_____
_____

Date:_____ Location:_____
_____
_____
_____
_____
_____
_____
_____
_____
_____

Date:_____ Location:_____

_____
_____
_____
_____
_____
_____
_____
_____
_____
_____

Date:_____ Location:_____

_____
_____
_____
_____
_____
_____
_____
_____
_____
_____

Date:_____ Location:_____

_____
_____
_____
_____
_____
_____
_____
_____
_____
_____

Date:_____ Location:_____

_____
_____
_____
_____
_____
_____
_____
_____
_____
_____

Date:_____ Location:_____

_____
_____
_____
_____
_____
_____
_____
_____
_____
_____
_____

Date:_____ Location:_____

_____
_____
_____
_____
_____
_____
_____
_____
_____
_____
_____

Date:_____ Location:_____

_____
_____
_____
_____
_____
_____
_____
_____
_____
_____
_____

Date:_____ Location:_____

_____
_____
_____
_____
_____
_____
_____
_____
_____
_____
_____

Date:_____ Location:_____

_____
_____
_____
_____
_____
_____
_____
_____
_____
_____

Date:_____ Location:_____

_____
_____
_____
_____
_____
_____
_____
_____
_____
_____

Date:_____ Location:_____

_____
_____
_____
_____
_____
_____
_____
_____
_____
_____

Date:_____ Location:_____

_____
_____
_____
_____
_____
_____
_____
_____
_____
_____

Date:_____ Location:_____

_____
_____
_____
_____
_____
_____
_____
_____
_____
_____

Date:_____ Location:_____

_____
_____
_____
_____
_____
_____
_____
_____
_____
_____

Date:_____ Location:_____

_____
_____
_____
_____
_____
_____
_____
_____
_____
_____

Date:_____ Location:_____

_____
_____
_____
_____
_____
_____
_____
_____
_____
_____

Date:_____ Location:_____

_____
_____
_____
_____
_____
_____
_____
_____
_____
_____

Date:_____ Location:_____

_____
_____
_____
_____
_____
_____
_____
_____
_____
_____

Date:_____ Location:_____

_____
_____
_____
_____
_____
_____
_____
_____
_____
_____

Date:_____ Location:_____

_____
_____
_____
_____
_____
_____
_____
_____
_____
_____

Date:_____ Location:_____

_____
_____
_____
_____
_____
_____
_____
_____
_____
_____
_____

Date:_____ Location:_____

_____
_____
_____
_____
_____
_____
_____
_____
_____
_____
_____

Date:_____ Location:_____

_____
_____
_____
_____
_____
_____
_____
_____
_____
_____
_____

Date:_____ Location:_____

_____
_____
_____
_____
_____
_____
_____
_____
_____
_____
_____

Date:_____ Location:_____

_____
_____
_____
_____
_____
_____
_____
_____
_____
_____

Date:_____ Location:_____

_____
_____
_____
_____
_____
_____
_____
_____
_____
_____

Date:_____ Location:_____

_____
_____
_____
_____
_____
_____
_____
_____
_____
_____

Date:_____ Location:_____

_____
_____
_____
_____
_____
_____
_____
_____
_____
_____

Section Six - Memories

- Your pages for SAR contacts, memories, or other information.

Made in the USA
San Bernardino, CA
26 May 2016